MW01055636

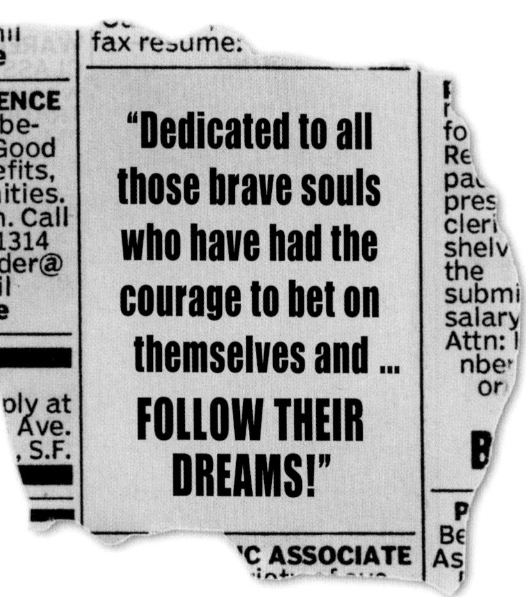
"Dedicated to all those brave souls who have had the courage to bet on themselves and ...
FOLLOW THEIR DREAMS!"

BY MAC ANDERSON

WHAT'S THE BIG IDEA?

The 10 Commandments for Business Success

Published by Simple Truths, LLC
1952 McDowell Road, Suite 300
Naperville, Illinois 60563

Toll Free 800-900-3427

Book Design: Vieceli Design Company, West Dundee, Illinois
Simple Truths is a registered trademark.
Printed and bound in the United States of America.

Editing by Alice Patenaude
Photography by iStockphoto.com and Getty Images

ISBN 978-1-60810-061-3

www.simpletruths.com

03 WOZ 10

Table of Contents

INTRODUCTION: What's the Big Idea?

by Mac Anderson

Ideas are powerful and one, just one, can change your business and your life. If you don't believe me, just pick up the phone and call Steve Jobs, Howard Schultz or Bill Gates. (Oops ... I just remembered, they might be pretty busy.) Here's the question and also the inspiration for this book: How do Big Ideas happen? Is there a process or a formula? Or do Big Ideas just "bubble up" when minds are curious and open to change?

As a lifetime entrepreneur, the "Big Idea question" has always fascinated me. Although every story is different, sometimes just reading how it happened can spark your imagination into action. Sometimes learning about how an individual who was willing to take the risk to follow his or her dream, and fight through adversity to keep it alive, might be the push you need. However, this collection of "Big Idea Stories" was not only written with the entrepreneur in mind, it was also written to inspire innovation within existing companies. Far too often, companies "roll on" with the status quo, only to wake up one day to find … competition has passed them by.

I know how one idea can change your life, because the "Successories idea" (in 1988) changed mine. The simple idea of taking a beautiful photograph, adding an inspirational quote and framing it for those who want to reinforce what they believe took off! It was so simple, that to this day, I find it hard to believe that no one had done it before us, but they hadn't. Our sales went from $5 million a year to $45 million in just three years, because of one very simple, but for us … **Big Idea**.

I truly respect those people and those companies with the courage to **take a risk** or **embrace change**, because risk and change are the common denominators for all Big Ideas. So with this little book, open your minds and prepare to be inspired. The next Big Idea could be yours!

All the Best,

Mac Anderson
Founder, Successories and Simple Truths

WHAT'S THE BIG IDEA?

The Ten Commandments for Business Success

By Mac Anderson "The Successories Story"

Big Ideas rarely happen overnight. They usually evolve from curious minds willing to take risks. At 41 years old, I had already enjoyed some success in business. When I was 27, I moved to Chicago from Kentucky to help Richard Kent launch Orval Kent Food Company as vice president of sales.

We took the company to $15 million in five years and I learned a lot along the way. It was a wonderful experience, but I had a burning desire to start my own company. The entrepreneurial bug had bitten and there was no turning back.

So in 1978, I started McCord (my middle name) Travel. Again the company did well,

but five years later I was approached to sell it, and did so. The travel business was interesting but I felt it was too difficult to differentiate ourselves from the competition. I was looking for a business that was unique, where I could add value through creativity.

When I sold McCord, I kept a small division of it that created custom recognition awards for our incentive travel clients. I also invited Mike McKee, my creative director, to join me in our quest to launch a new recognition award company that we would differentiate through our creativity. I knew this was a business I could get excited about because I truly believed that creating a recognition culture was critical to any company's success. I also believed in Mike McKee. Not only was he a very

talented artist and designer, he was also a great person. The synergy worked and we made a good team.

One of our recognition customers was a large automotive company. When supplying the awards for their dealer conference, they asked if we had anything with a motivational theme to leave at each plate. I said that over the years I had collected what I thought were motivating quotes. We could create a little book with these quotes, and hopefully, they'd like it. They said... "Let's do it!"

The next day, our phone rang off the hook with hundreds of dealers wanting to purchase more copies to give to their sales people and to use as customer gifts. I thought, "Wow... people like quotes just like I do!" I began to wonder... would other people actually want to buy this little book? To find out, I took a dozen books to three hotel gift shops and said, "I'll actually give you these books if you'll try to sell them by the register on a little plastic easel for $6.95." They said, "We'll give it a shot." (The margins were good!)

"Wow... people like quotes just like I do!"

— Mac Anderson

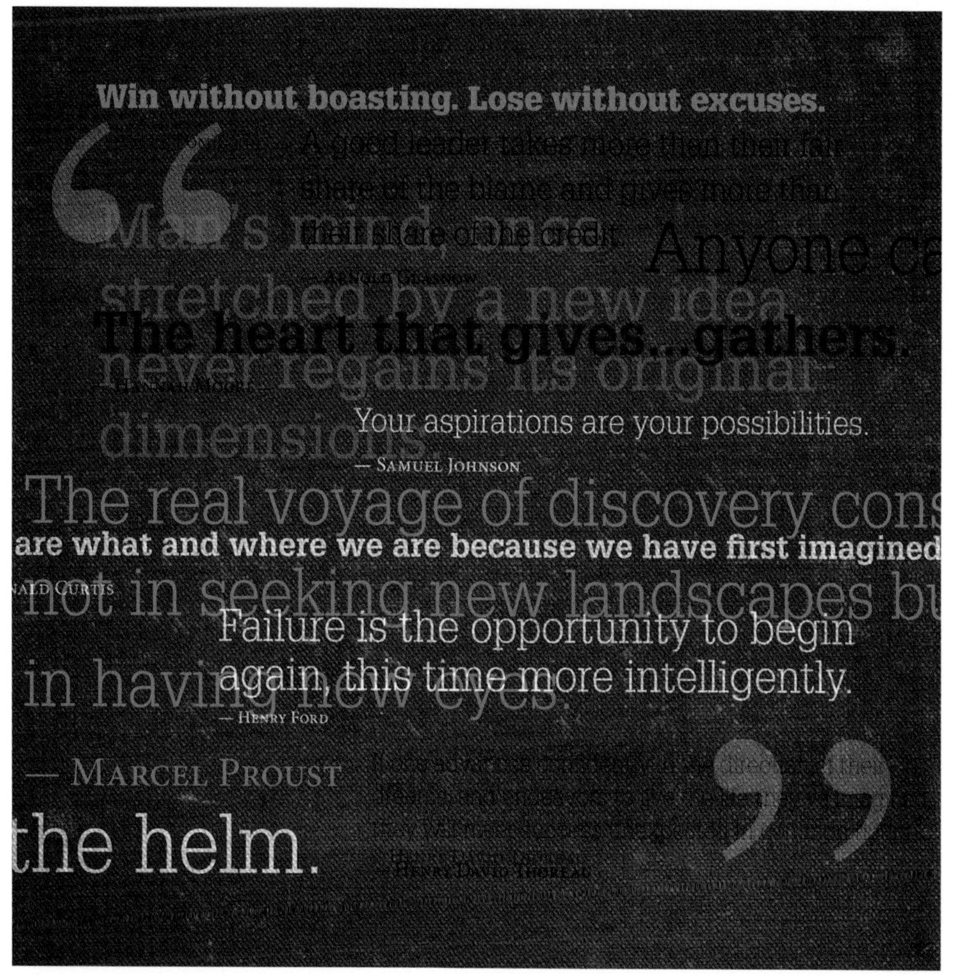
Win without boasting. Lose without excuses.
A good leader takes more than their fair share of the blame and gives more than their share of the credit.
Man's mind, once stretched by a new idea never regains its original dimensions.
Anyone ca
The heart that gives...gathers.
Your aspirations are your possibilities.
— Samuel Johnson
The real voyage of discovery cons
are what and where we are because we have first imagined
not in seeking new landscapes bu
in having new eyes.
— Marcel Proust
Failure is the opportunity to begin again, this time more intelligently.
— Henry Ford
the helm.
— Henry David Thoreau

When I returned a week later, all the books were gone. In fact most, they said, had sold in the first two days. People really did like quotes! Other hotel gift shops began to sell the book and airport shops quickly picked up on the idea. The rocket had been launched and over the next 18 months, we sold 800,000 little books with the simple title, *Motivational Quotes*.

Almost a year into our launch of the book, I had another idea. I wondered... would people want to hang quotes on their walls? To find out, I put a photo of a brass plaque with a quote in the back of each book. I also included an order form next to the photo that said, "Order your favorite quote from this book on a plaque for $19.95." Well, the orders rolled in quickly, and many times people didn't order just one. They ordered 25, 50, even 100 to give as gifts to their teams and to their customers.

By now I think you're beginning to get the picture. The idea for building a business around selling quotation products was rapidly gathering steam. The train was beginning to leave the station!

Therefore, Successories evolved from a little book titled, *Motivational Quotes*, to brass plaques selling for

$19.95, to what was our breakthrough idea of combining beautiful photographs with words to reinforce corporate values and personal goals. In this case, as in most Big Ideas, success didn't come cascading like Niagara Falls, it came one drop at a time.

In hindsight, what was amazing about this idea was its simplicity. How could anything be more simple than to find a beautiful photo, add a theme, a quote and sell it as wall décor? The theme for our first catalog was "Decorate Your Walls With Great Ideas" and our slogan was "Our

> *"... I knew then I had a tiger by the tail."*
>
> *— Mac Anderson*

Goal Is to Help You Reach Yours." Companies and individuals got it almost instantly. When we placed our first ad in an airline magazine, our phones were jammed for three weeks. I knew then I had a "tiger by the tail."

What surprised me, however, were the types of customers that were placing orders. We had developed the products primarily for companies to hang in their common areas, but we quickly discovered that individuals from all walks of life wanted the opportunity to hang something beautiful on their walls that would reinforce their personal goals and core beliefs. School teachers, sales people, entrepreneurs, coaches and even parents called by the thousands to decorate their walls with great ideas. In fact, at one point in the early '90s, we were shipping over 2,000 packages a day of framed wall décor. Within five years, our sales were over $50 million a year. We owned this small niche of motivational wall décor and no competition was over $1 million in sales.

> How did it happen?
> What were some of the key challenges
> and choices along the way?

RULE #1

EXPECT ADVERSITY

Big Ideas and adversity are joined at the hip. Lots of people have great ideas, but turning them into reality is, well, difficult because the road to reality is loaded with potholes, roadblocks and detours. It is filled with choices, tough choices that can make or break your dream. But I've learned that in business, and in life, anything worthwhile is never easy. When you can look back after fighting through the challenges and the adversity and say… "I did it!" there is no better feeling in the world.

In bringing Big Ideas to life, you'll usually face two types of adversity. The first is what I'll call "learning curve stuff." The second, however, is more serious. Let's just call it "near death moments." At Successories we had plenty of both.

Keep in mind there are no "how-to manuals" to read if you are the first to do something, so you must expect the unexpected. In fact, I've often said that starting a new company is like going through a maze. You take a few steps forward, hit the wall, you go sideways a few steps, hit the wall again, go back five steps and start again until you begin to see the light at the end of the tunnel. At first, you think you know where the path will lead, but it usually takes some dangerous turns along the way. Of course, that's what risk is all about.

We knew that the idea of motivational wall décor was a good one, but how could we build a substantial business and a brand that would allow us to become the unquestioned leader in this new niche? Looking back, there were many learning curve challenges along the way, but our first one was pretty basic. How could we ship thousands of framed prints without laminating them or breaking the glass? It may sound simple, but it wasn't. We went through many packaging designs and framing options, to minimize breakage. We also discovered that in some instances, the package would leave our plant in perfect condition, but the humidity (in transit) would cause the print to swell enough to rub against the glass and create "spots." In the end, it took lots of money, headaches, and trial and error to get it right.

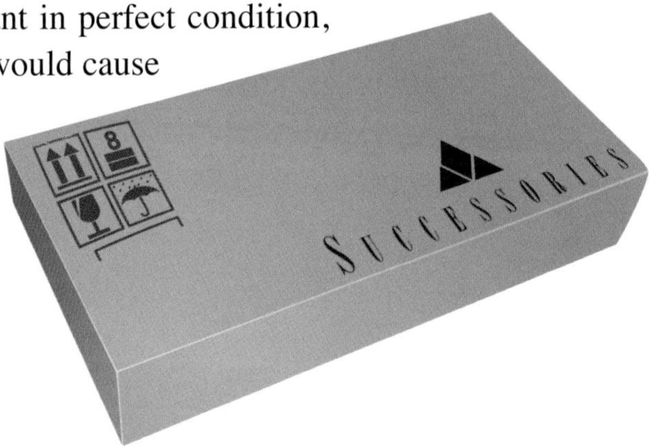

We also went through many other challenges in the early stages:

* **Protecting our trademarks and copyrights from copycats.**

* **Automating our framing production and shipping.**

* **Getting our accounting systems in place.**

* **Financing our rapid growth. In less than five years, we grew to over $50 million in sales.**

* **Hiring the right people for key positions.**

All of these things presented tremendous challenges in a rapid growth situation. However, in the fall of 1993, we experienced our "near death moment." The company had gone from $5 million to $45 million in only three years. We were on a roll, but in the summer of '93, we decided to install new software to connect shipping with accounting. It was a big job, but we felt we could finish it before our busy holiday season. Unfortunately, in June of 1993, our CFO was diagnosed with terminal brain cancer. He was only 47 years old, and I was devastated for him and his family. Because of Jim's illness, the project got delayed and dramatically hindered our ability to ship our orders during the holiday season. It was an entrepreneur's nightmare, and when the dust settled in January of 1994, the news was bad. We were faced with devastating financial losses, and the banks, who had financed our growth, wanted us to raise new capital to pay off our debt. In the end, we survived this disaster, but for me, there were many anxious moments and sleepless nights over the next year.

"We were faced with devastating financial losses, and the banks, who had financed our growth, wanted us to raise new capital to pay off our debt."

— Mac Anderson

THE CRITICAL CHOICES WE MADE

In the end, your success in business, as in life, will be determined by choices you make. Will you make mistakes and poor choices occasionally? Of course you will. One of my all-time favorite quotes is from Henry Ford who said, "Failure is only the opportunity to begin again more intelligently." Likewise there will be many "new beginnings" when bringing Big Ideas to life. In looking back at any successful business, you can identify some critical choices along the way.

At Successories, I feel these seven choices were the most important:

* Choosing a product that I could be passionate about

My purpose was to try to make a positive difference in what I felt was a pretty negative world. My passion and unwavering belief in what we were doing was the fuel that helped conquer the many obstacles we faced along the way.

* Choosing a great creative partner

Mike McKee took my good ideas and made them great, with design.

---

* Choosing quality as the "mother" and never mess with mom!

Our paper stock, framing material, photographs, and even our packaging was of the highest quality. It was one of our core values. Even in tough times when we needed to cut our costs, we never sacrificed the quality of our products.

---

* Choosing a great name for the company

The name, Successories, was unique and memorable. It perfectly captured what we were trying to do and helped us build a well-known brand known for quality and creativity.

---

* Choosing to sell proprietary products only

We wanted to control our quality and our pricing; therefore, we decided to create all of our products and product designs internally. We also chose not to sell our products through other retail channels; therefore, if you liked what we did, you had to purchase from us.

---

* Choosing to narrow our focus

There was the temptation to sell motivational products from other companies. Since we had created a unique distribution channel, we were constantly bombarded by other companies who wanted us to sell their products. We resisted that temptation, and it helped make our brand unique.

---

* Choosing not to quit when times got tough

If someone were to ask me to pick one word to describe any success I've enjoyed in my life, I wouldn't hesitate. The word would be ... **perseverance**.

What I just shared is a snapshot of how my Big Idea evolved. But my goal in this book is to share much more than "my story." My goal is to share many "Big Idea stories," and then have you look back and reflect on what these stories have in common. What are some of the common denominators of the evolution of Big Ideas?

So whether you're an entrepreneur, a "wanna be entrepreneur," or a manager looking for that next Big Idea ... this book is for you. As I mentioned in my introduction, every "Big Idea story" is different, and sometimes just reading how it happened can spark your imagination into action.

SO READ ON AND ... LET THE SPARKS FLY!

Howard Schultz has Changed the Way Americans Drink Coffee

From a morning latte to a Frappuccino® pick-me-up, a trip to Starbucks is now part of the daily routine for millions of people around the world. For Howard Schultz, the visionary who changed the way Americans drink coffee, it's a Big Idea that became reality for a kid who was raised in a Brooklyn, New York, housing project.

As the oldest of three children in a working-class family, Howard grew up quickly. By the time he was 16-years old, he had an after-school job stretching animal skins at a furrier in the garment district of Manhattan. A natural athlete, Howard was offered a football scholarship at Northern Michigan University, where he majored in communications.

Finding Your Passion … Sometimes It Takes Awhile

Howard became the first in his family to graduate from college. But, unsure of his career direction, Howard worked at a ski lodge for a year before accepting a position in Xerox's sales training program. There, he learned sales, marketing and presentation techniques, and made 50 cold calls a day.

In his book, *Pour Your Heart Into It: How Starbucks Built a Company One Cup at a Time*, by Howard Schultz, with Dori Jones Yang, Howard recalls that his sales career was great preparation for his future:

> **"Cold-calling was great training for business. It taught me to think on my feet. So many doors slammed on me that I had to develop a thick skin and a concise sales pitch … "**

"By the Third Sip, I Was Hooked"

Looking for more challenge in his career, Howard moved to Perstorp, a Swedish company, and was eventually put in charge of U.S. operations for its Hammarplast housewares subsidiary. It was there he discovered a small retailer in Seattle, the Starbucks Coffee, Tea and Spice company, that was placing unusually large orders for a certain type of drip coffeemaker. Howard decided to investigate for himself.

"The minute the door opened, a heady aroma of coffee reached out and drew me in … By the third sip, I was hooked."

Howard met with Starbucks' owners, Jerry Baldwin and Gordon Bowker, who were managing their business with the sole purpose of maximizing the quality of the coffee beans they sold to their customers.

On the five-hour trip back to New York the next day, Howard couldn't stop thinking about Starbucks.

"I believe in destiny. At that moment, flying 35,000 feet above the earth, I could feel the tug of Starbucks. There was something magical about it, a passion and authenticity I had never experienced in business."

Despite his passion for the company, it took Howard a year to convince Starbucks' owner Jerry Baldwin to hire him, overcoming objections that his vision and style might clash with the culture of the company.

A Vision is Born

Finally, in 1982, Howard took a huge pay cut to become Starbucks' head of marketing and accepted a small equity share as one of its owners.

"My parents could not understand what it was that attracted me to Starbucks. I left a well paying, prestigious job to join what was then a small Seattle retailer with five stores. For my part, I saw Starbucks not for what it was, but for what it could be. It had immediately captivated me with its combination of passion and authenticity. If it could expand nationwide, romancing the Italian artistry of espresso-making as well as offering fresh-roasted beans, I gradually realized, it could reinvent an age-old commodity and appeal to millions of people as strongly as it appealed to me."

"Starbucks had missed the point—completely missed it."

— Howard Schultz

At that time, Starbucks only sold great coffee beans—not coffee by the cup. It was during a trip to Italy where Howard experienced the coffee bar atmosphere of neighbors gathering together to share espresso and conversation, that he had an epiphany about the direction of the company:

"Starbucks had missed the point—completely missed it. What we had to do was un-

lock the personal relationship that people could have to coffee, its social aspect. I couldn't believe that Starbucks was in the coffee business, yet was overlooking so central an element of it."

Changing the Way Americans Drink Coffee

Upon returning to work, Howard shared his idea, one that could *"serve as the foundation for a whole new industry and change the way Americans drank coffee."* But the idea fell on deaf ears. Starbucks' owners viewed the company as a retailer, not a restaurant, and felt a change in direction would dilute the integrity of what they envisioned the mission of a coffee store to be.

It took Howard nearly a year to convince the owners to test the idea of serving espresso in one of Starbucks' stores—in a 300-square-foot space that included no chairs. It was soon jammed with customers and by closing time, the store served almost double the amount of customers of its best-performing store.

Despite the obvious customer interest, Starbucks' owners still viewed serving espresso drinks as a distraction from the stores' core business of selling coffee beans. An impasse had been reached. After talking with

friends about the idea of going independent to open espresso bars, Howard knew what he had to do:

Step Out of Your Comfort Zone

"This is my moment. If I don't use the opportunity, if I don't step out of my comfort zone and risk it all, if I let too much time tick on, my moment will pass. I knew that if I didn't take advantage of this opportunity, I would replay it in my mind for my whole life, wondering: What if? Why didn't I? This was my shot. Even if it didn't work, I still had to try it."

So, despite the fact that he just learned that his wife, Sheri, was pregnant, Howard decided to start his own company—Il Giornale, mirroring the name of the largest daily newspaper in Italy, which he hoped would result in daily coffee sales—using Starbucks coffee, of course!

Starbucks' owner Jerry Baldwin became Il Giornale's first investor, backing Howard's new business with $150,000. Howard focused all of his energy on acquiring investors for his new company and his first Il Giornale opened in 1986.

SCHULTZ'S BIG IDEA?

Serving espresso in one of Starbucks' stores—

in a 300-square-foot space that included no chairs. It was soon jammed with customers and by closing time, the store served almost double the amount of customers of its best performing store.

Find Colleagues Who Share Your Values

While sales exceeded expectations, cash flow was still tight. Howard realized that he needed help for Il Giornale's network of coffee bars to become a reality. He found the perfect partner in Dave Olsen, who ran his own coffee café and who had ten years of espresso experience.

> *"If you're building an organization, you realize quickly that you can't do it alone. You'll build a much stronger company if you can find a colleague you trust absolutely, someone who brings different strengths to the mix but who still shares your values."*

Howard expanded his team and his Il Giornale stores, but in 1987, he learned that the owners of Starbucks were going to sell their stores, the roasting plant and the Starbucks' name.

Even though Starbucks had annual sales many times that of Il Giornale's three stores, Howard knew he had to buy Starbucks. But that meant raising an additional $3.8 million. Howard met with his investors and offered them a chance to invest in the Starbucks' purchase. They backed him and by August of 1987, the purchase was complete.

Staying with the Starbucks' Name

"For most entrepreneurs who have founded their first company, giving up its name is like throwing away their baby. I certainly felt attached to Il Giornale, which I had created out of nothing. But the Starbucks' name was so much better known, and I knew in my heart that it was the right choice."

Now, as Starbucks, Howard's original goal of opening 125 stores within five years was finally within reach. Today, Starbucks company-owned stores exist in 43 countries outside the United States. But it all began with Howard's Big Idea to create a network of stores providing just the right experience for customers to enjoy the bold flavor of espresso.

Jump When There's An Idea Others Don't See

"Part of what constitutes success is timing and chance. But most of us have to create our own opportunities and be prepared to jump when we see a big one others can't see.

"It's one thing to dream, but when the moment is right, you've got to be willing to leave what's familiar and go out to find your own sound. That's what I did in 1985. If I hadn't, Starbucks wouldn't be what it is today."

Debbi Fields' Secret Ingredients for Success

Mrs. Fields Cookies' Interesting Marketing Strategy

Debbi Fields opened her first cookie store in Palo Alto, California, in 1977, as a young mother with no business experience. How did she do it? In many ways, she defied business logic. She never spent money on advertising and gave away her cookies for free!

FREE
COOKIES
TODAY

The roots of her success—her appreciation for her customers and her cookie recipe—stemmed from her childhood. As a teenager, she'd held a variety of different jobs: chasing foul balls for the Oakland A's baseball team, working as a retail store clerk and Christmas elf, performing with dolphins at Sea World and serving as a governess to five children. But, delivering great customer service was at the heart of all of her experiences. In her autobiography, *One Smart Cookie: How a Housewife's Chocolate Chip Recipe Turned Into a Multimillion-Dollar Business—The Story of Mrs. Fields Cookies*, with Alan Furst, Debbi describes how even as a retail clerk, she realized that it was a key to success.

"I could see the response when the customers realized that somebody, even a fifteen-year-old, part-time sales clerk, cared about making things easy and pleasant for them."

— Debbi Fields

Great Customer Service Is a Key Ingredient

"If people didn't see something they wanted, I'd go into the stockroom and bring it out. I could see the response when the customers realized that somebody, even a fifteen-year-old, part-time sales clerk, cared about making things easy and pleasant for them. Gradually, it became clear to me that they were delighted with such service, because they weren't getting it wherever else they shopped."

Debbi came from a family of five children and as the baby of the family, sometimes it was tough to distinguish herself from sisters who were athletic and competitive. But Debbi's talents shone in the kitchen. Baking chocolate chip cookies was an easy project for a rainy afternoon. Debbi spent a lot of time experimenting with the recipe. By the time she was 17, she'd discovered that the secret of the cookie lay more in the quality of its original ingredients than in any variation of the formula.

When she was 18, she met her future husband, Randy Fields, a prominent economist. After their marriage, she grew tired of not having her own ambition and answering "housewife" to the question of "what do you do?" at cocktail parties with her husband.

"I liked making people happy. It was the one thing under the sun that I knew was right, and it was something that I'd always been able to do—I simply understood people in that particular way. It wasn't anything so complicated as a talent or a skill. It was an instinct, and all it took was the desire to do it. I need to share something of myself with the world. I wanted to give, to be part of things. And what I happened to have available for giving was a pretty darn good chocolate chip cookie. So to me, selling cookies in a store was a good idea."

Persevering Despite Naysayers

However, everyone she talked with disagreed. Her husband pointed her in the direction of market analysis, but they all said the same thing. America loves crispy cookies, but hers were soft and chewy.

Debbi's own personal analysis showed different results. Her cookies disappeared whenever she made them. In fact, her husband's clients began to call and see if she was going to bake some of her cookies when they were visiting with him. But, these clients were also naysayers to her business idea, even as their mouths were stuffed with cookies.

"All the professionals were negative and it made me crazy. I couldn't understand it. I knew I wasn't sophisticated, but I had eyes to see with. It was like they were telling me one thing, yet showing me something completely opposite."

So she got the opinions of her parents and in-laws and her friends. But while they loved her cookies, they thought making a business from them was entirely another matter.

"All the professionals were negative and it made me crazy."

— Debbi Fields

Every Good Idea Starts Out as Someone's Crazy Dream

"I became, I'm afraid, one of those terrible pests with an idea burning in their brain that they can't get rid of, yet can't put into action. There's a tendency to laugh at such people, to congratulate ourselves that, whatever other difficulties we have in our lives, at least we aren't deluded. And the funny part is that we know, absolutely know, because the examples are everywhere, that just about every good idea in the world started out as somebody's crazy dream."

Even her husband had his doubts about the success of her business idea, but he talked with the banker who had made the couple's home loan and was willing to back Debbi's business idea with his own money. So the papers were signed and at 20 years old, Debbi Fields was in the cookie business.

Finding the Critical Principle that Defines a Business

With Debbi's youth and a great product, she knew she was on the right track. She also knew that there was something that would define her business.

"The third thing I had going for me was just as important as the product, maybe even more. It was the critical principle that would build the business and determine all its policies. It was the guiding light that led Mrs. Fields Cookies into the success it would later achieve. I had no idea what it was or that I had it.

"Is that unusual? I suspect it isn't. A number of people who have created successful enterprises will cheerfully admit they had no idea what they were doing when they started out. And they will add that certain special thing, something of which they were entirely unaware, and that

really made the difference. The trick is that you can't find the hidden treasure until you start digging. Often enough, if you take the leap and do something, something will happen. Probably not what you thought, but something."

Creating a Customer Experience

In Debbi's case, that "something" turned out to be the experience she had wanted to deliver to her customers as a teenager. *"I realized I wasn't going into business to make money, that Randy's clients and my friends and both our families and lots of bankers were right in their belief that you didn't sell cookies in order to get rich. I didn't care about the money. It was an experience I wanted to create, some kind of gift to people—a lot of whom I felt were exactly like me, cheated of the emotional value of their money by big stores, fast food, systems without affection."*

After finding a location that appealed to her instincts and with the help of her family and others to equip and decorate her new store, Debbi launched her business as Mrs. Fields Chocolate Chippery.

On her first day of business, she laid out the cookies and while a few people stopped in to check out the cookies, they smiled and walked away —without buying a single cookie! So, she took her cookies out to the street for people to sample.

Giving Cookies Away for Free!

"*If I can't sell them, I'm going to give them away. What I'd done, in that moment, was add the critical component to a business that would, in a few years' time, grow to over a hundred million dollars a year, but I didn't know that. It was just an instinct, of the try-anything variety, but what made the difference was that I was willing to try anything.*"

When tasting the free cookie, customers not only asked where they could buy them, but came back repeatedly.

Do What You Love to Do

"In truth, I did not find success because I wasn't looking for it. What I wanted was to be allowed to do the thing in the world that I did best—which I believed then and believe now is the greatest privilege there is. When I did that, success found me. If you chase it, you'll never catch it. But if you do what you love to do, and do it as well as you know in your heart you can, it will eventually show up. When you least expect it. When, often enough, you've given up all hope of its ever arriving."

Fred Smith Guarantees Overnight Delivery

Federal Express fills the need for reliable overnight service around the world

★ ★ ★ ★ ★

A pioneer in overnight package delivery, Federal Express founder Fred Smith's passion for airplanes and flying began early in life. Learning to fly at age 15, he was already piloting a candidate running in the Tennessee gubernatorial primary race to campaign stops by the time he was 17.

★ ★ ★ ★ ★

A Term Paper ... His Business Plan?

It was at Yale University in 1965, where Fred first got the idea for a delivery system that would revolutionize the way business is conducted. In a term paper he wrote for an economics class, Fred described a "hub and spoke" concept for a delivery service, with the "hub" in middle America and the "spokes" radiating out to other cities.

Similar to a telephone network, Fred outlined how packages could be flown into the hub, sorted and sent out before dawn—with packages delivered overnight. While it's reported that Fred only received a grade of "C" on his paper, it outlined his business idea for an airfreight system that could accommodate time-sensitive shipments.

Unreliable Deliveries Prompt Action

After graduating with a degree in economics, Fred served in the U.S. Marines and returned to Little Rock, Arkansas, to buy controlling interest in Arkansas Aviation Sales. As the son of the founder of the Dixie Greyhound Bus Line and the Toddle House chain of fast-food restaurants, Fred relied heavily on his family's fortune in all of his business ventures. In his book, *Overnight Success: Federal Express and Frederick Smith, Its Renegade Creator,* author Vance Trimble describes Fred's reaction to the tremendous difficulty he had in getting packages and other airfreight delivered within one to two days during his days at Arkansas Aviation Sales.

> *"We can't count on getting any air freight shipment on a timely and reliable basis. It's just unpredictable. Somebody ought to do something about it!"*

What Fred did first was to look into getting his first two Falcon jets at a bargain price. He investigated using his planes as an air courier service for bonds, the U.S. mail service and the Federal Reserve. None of these deals initially came through.

So, Fred began to draw upon that college term paper to create a customized delivery system.

"For our network, I used as a model the economic activity of the Federal Reserve banking system, because it was in those days a perfect model of the economic activity in the U.S. And that's where the Federal Express name came from. It just stuck in my mind.

I wanted something that sounded substantial and nationwide," Fred told a *BusinessWeek* Bureau Chief in 2004.

Overcoming Obstacles

Fred founded the Federal Express Corporation in 1971. To launch his delivery network, Fred needed to overcome a number of obstacles including government regulations that restricted the weight of air taxis, and securing the funding to purchase planes and retool them to carry only cargo.

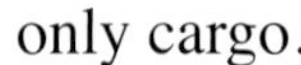

He commissioned several feasibility studies to help him lure investors. They confirmed Fred's idea that there was a real business need for an air express package service and that users not only wanted their packages to travel overnight, they wanted them to be promptly delivered by ground courier. Launching a business with planes and trucks combined as part of one delivery system required a lot of up-front capital... a difference from most start-up businesses. Fred drew upon his own money as well as his family's fortune, as he sought investors to take a gamble on a faster, more dependable delivery service that could revolutionize business practices.

When the government weight regulation was lifted, Fred again bid for U.S. mail contracts and later spread the word that Federal Express planes could also deliver packages overnight.

A Sparse Opening Night

Federal Express finally launched its overnight package delivery service from its Memphis "hub" on March 12, 1973. Its service to seven other cities yielded just six packages the first night. Expanding his network to 25 cities with 14 planes, Fred launched his service again a month later, this time netting 186 packages, making April 17, 1973, Federal Express' official birthday.

"It was easy to demonstrate how we'd do once we broke even, but it still took us 26 months and losses of $29 million to do so."

— Fred Smith

In addition to an initial small package volume, cash flow proved to be a consistent issue for the newly launched Federal Express. To keep the company running, Fred made a few sketchy business decisions, even flying to Las Vegas and using his winnings to meet the Federal Express payroll.

"I was in Chicago when I was turned down for the umpteenth time for a (loan) source. I went to the airport to go back to Memphis, and saw on the TWA schedule a flight to Las Vegas. I won $27,000, starting with a couple of hundred and sent it back to Memphis. The $27,000 wasn't decisive, but it was an omen that things would get better."

Federal Express Finally Turns Profitable

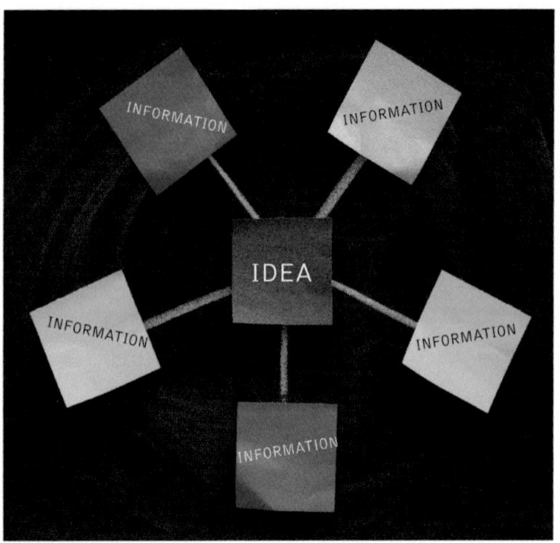

Despite many rocky false starts with investors, Federal Express began to turn the corner on profitability.

"It was easy to demonstrate how we'd do once we broke even, but it still took us 26 months and losses of $29 million to do so," Fred told *Fortune Small Business* in 2002.

The company reached a turning point as Federal Express had its first profitable month in July 1975.

As his company grew, on its way to becoming the world's largest express transportation company, Fred continued to rely on his intuition and research in generating Big Ideas. He estimated that throughout the 1980s, he spent at least four hours a day reading—newspapers, magazines, books on management theory and flight theory and journals on the latest technological developments.

Timing and Vision—Two Keys of a Successful Business

"The common trait of people who supposedly have vision is that they spend a lot of time reading and gathering information, and then synthesize it until they come up with an idea.

"Timing? Yes, very important—knowing when to really go, and when to sit on the sidelines. Once you decide to go, certainly serendipity plays a big part in it. But I think timing is often more important than luck.

"In my case, for example, the idea that is Federal Express absolutely, positively would not have worked five years before we did it, for many reasons. And five years later the market would have been so clear that somebody would have served it in one way or another. And that is probably true of most start-up organizations."

Herb Kelleher Proposes New Intrastate Airline

Southwest Airlines is born from a drawing on a cocktail napkin

It takes a lot to get a new airline off the ground. But a business idea drawn on a cocktail napkin? That was the legendary start of Southwest Airlines back in 1966 when Rollin King, a San Antonio entrepreneur who owned a small commuter airline, proposed the idea of an intrastate airline to Herb Kelleher, a New Jersey bred lawyer, who did work for Rollin's firm.

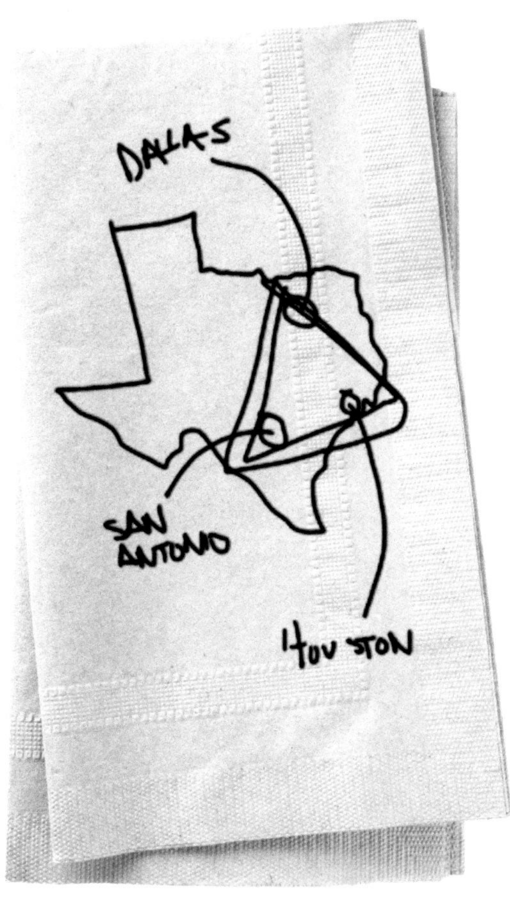

Drawing a triangle on that cocktail napkin, Rollin outlined an idea that he and his banker, John Parker, had come up with, providing air service to the Golden Triangle of Texas—Houston, Dallas and San Antonio—an area that was experiencing rapid economic and population growth.

In their book, *Nuts! Southwest Airlines' Crazy Recipe for Business and Personal Success*, authors Kevin and Jackie Freiberg recounted the conversation:

"Herb, let's start an airline."

"Rollin, you're crazy. Let's do it!"

That was the easy part. Herb filed the paperwork to incorporate Southwest while King, with a contribution from Herb, worked to raise the capital and the political support for the new airline.

Holding Their Own Against the Competition

But the existing airlines weren't pleased about a newcomer on their turf, and after the application for Southwest to fly between the three cities was approved, they launched a legal battle in an attempt to keep the new airline grounded.

Braniff, Trans Texas (later Texas International) and Continental Airlines first tried to get a restraining order against Southwest. The trial court ruled that Dallas, Houston and San Antonio were adequately served by existing carriers. It took seven months for Southwest's appeal to make it to the state court of civil appeals.

By this point, the original investors' money was being eaten up in legal expenses and some of Southwest's board of directors thought the strength of the major carriers might be insurmountable in launching the new airline.

A Personal Commitment to Southwest

But not Herb Kelleher. His personal belief in Southwest prompted him to take an even more personal stake in the outcome of the fledgling airline:

"Gentlemen, let's go one more round with them. I will continue to represent the company in court, and I'll postpone any legal fees and pay every cent of the court costs out of my own pocket."

Herb argued Southwest's case before the Texas Supreme Court, which overturned the lower appellate court's decision, giving Southwest its certificate to fly.

But the legal battles were hardly over. Braniff, Texas International and Continental appealed to the U.S. Supreme Court, but the Court refused to hear the appeal.

The major carriers refused to give up. In fact, when Southwest set its launch date, two major carriers filed a court injunction to stop it from initiating service. Herb worked all night to prepare his case and the Texas Supreme Court ruled in Southwest's favor.

Herb called Lamar Muse, who was then CEO of the new airline, telling him to go ahead with Southwest's scheduled flight no matter what:

"Lamar said, 'Gee, Herb, what do I do? Suppose the sheriff shows up and tries to prevent the flight?'

"So I said, 'Leave tire tracks on his shirt. We're going, come hell or high water.'"

In all, Herb represented Southwest Airlines in 31 separate administrative and/or judicial proceedings with those carriers over four or five years, including three trips to the U.S. Supreme Court.

Southwest Finally Takes to the Air

On June 18, 1971, Southwest Airlines was in the air and began to distinguish itself in the airline industry through its low fares, creative advertising and the unique esprit de corps that is the hallmark of Southwest's culture.

To compete with the established carriers, Southwest continually looked for innovative ways to differentiate the new airline. Its consistently low fares allowed more people to fly. But because it had just three planes at the time, Southwest had to find a way to avoid cutting back its schedule. The solution? The 10-minute turnaround, where ground crews ready the plane for its next flight in under ten minutes.

People Come First

Herb became chairman of Southwest in 1978, while still focusing on his legal duties. It wasn't until 1982 that he became CEO of Southwest. As a co-founder of the company, he infused a commitment to people throughout the organization. It's a trait he learned from his mother, who taught him that positions and titles are meaningless and everyone should be treated with respect.

"I always felt that our people came first. *Some of the business schools regarded that as a conundrum. They would say: Which comes first, your people, your customers, or your shareholders? And I would say, it's not a conundrum. Your people come first, and if you treat them right, they'll treat the customers right, and the customers will come back, and that'll make the shareholders happy,"* Herb told *BusinessWeek*.

Southwest's commitment to its people is displayed in many ways, from becoming the first in the airline industry to start a profit-sharing plan to encouraging employee ideas without levels of bureaucracy or retribution for a failed idea.

> *"We look for attitudes, people with a sense of humor who don't take themselves too seriously. We'll train you on whatever it is you have to do..."*
>
> *— Herb Kelleher*

"You've got to take the time to listen to people's ideas. If you just tell somebody no, that's an act of power and, in my opinion, an abuse of power. You don't want to constrain people in their thinking." Herb told *Fortune Magazine* reporter Katrina Brooker in a 2001 interview.

Life's Too Short Not To Be Humorous

Herb also was committed to creating an atmosphere of having fun as part of Southwest's culture.

"Life is too short and too hard and too serious not to be humorous about it. We look for attitudes, people with a sense of humor who don't take themselves too seriously. We'll train you on whatever it is you have to do, but the one thing Southwest cannot change in people is inherent attitudes."

Southwest Airlines was successful by concentrating on its niche—providing the best service and lowest fares to its high-frequency travelers. The company has been obsessed with keeping costs low to maximize profitability rather than increasing market share. Herb believed that confusing the two has kept many firms from fulfilling their fundamental purpose.

Focusing on Profitability

"Market share has nothing to do with profitability. Market share says we just want to be big; we don't care if we make money doing it. That's what misled much of the airline industry for fifteen years, after deregulation."

Southwest Airlines became profitable in 1973. Starting as an idea on a cocktail napkin, Southwest Airlines now has more than 500 planes and flies more than 100 million passengers a year. Herb Kelleher's respect for people, persistence and innovation were instrumental in Southwest's success.

"We never tried to be like other airlines. From the very beginning, we told our people, 'Question it. Challenge it. Remember, decades of conventional wisdom have sometimes led the airline industry into huge losses.'

"This is a company created by its people. It is a daily celebration of our customers. It is a daily celebration of great employees."

BOOKS

Jeff Bezos Takes on Traditional Brick and Mortar Book Stores

Amazon.com helps change the face of publishing using the Internet

Today, consumers across the world think nothing of doing their shopping at their keyboards in their pajamas during the middle of the night. But in 1995, e-commerce was in its infancy and entrepreneur Jeff Bezos was ready to launch something the world had never seen before—an online bookseller that would forever change how merchants do business.

Jeff's interest in computers began in his youth with the science projects he always had in the garage, from an amateur radio to an old Hoover vacuum cleaner that was converted into a hovercraft. He planned on being an astronaut or a physicist, but after graduating as his high school's valedictorian, he chose to study electrical engineering and business administration at Princeton.

Jeff was a sought-after college graduate, working at his first jobs in the financial arena. But it wasn't until Jeff accepted a position at D.E. Shaw, a firm that specialized in applying computer science to stock market trading, that he began to dream of making an impact on his own.

A Big Idea Takes Shape

While at D.E. Shaw, Jeff was asked to investigate business possibilities for the newly burgeoning Internet. His research revealed that Internet usage was growing at an astonishing rate of 2,300 percent a year. Jeff looked at the top 20 products that could be sold on the Web... and books were at the top of the list.

The Internet offered possibilities for book sales that traditional brick and mortar stores did not—an unlimited number of books that could be available through the Web's search and retrieval technology for a virtually limitless number of people. Using a centralized ordering and distribution location, Jeff reasoned that an online bookseller could be run more economically than the largest traditional bookseller.

Walking Away From a Secure Corporate Career

He made a recommendation to D. E. Shaw to sell books online, but the idea was rejected. Despite the promise of a lucrative career, Jeff wanted to resign from the firm to start his own Internet bookselling company.

Jeff's boss emphasized the financial security he would be giving up and asked him to think about his decision. In his book, *Amazon.com Get Big Fast*, author Robert Spector shared Jeff's thought process:

> **"I knew that when I was 80 there was no chance that I would regret having walked away from my 1994 Wall Street bonus in the middle of the year. I wouldn't even have remembered that. But I did think there was a chance that I might regret significantly not participating in this thing called the Internet, that I believed passionately in. I also knew that if I had tried and failed, I wouldn't regret that. So, once I thought about it that way, it became incredibly easy to make that decision."**

> *"When something is growing 2,300 percent a year, you have to move fast."*
>
> *— Jeff Bezos, CEO Amazon.com*

So, Jeff decided to head west to launch his new venture. He chose Seattle because of its access to programming talent . . . and because it was a short drive from the Ingram Book Group, which ran the largest book distribution center in the United States.

Jeff moved quickly on laying the foundation for his new business. "*When something is growing 2,300 percent a year, you have to move fast. A sense of urgency becomes your most valuable asset.*"

Choosing the Right Company Name

While Jeff's wife, MacKenzie, drove their car toward Seattle, Jeff worked on a first draft of the company's business plan on his laptop. Jeff had decided to call his new company Cadabra, Inc. (as in Abracadabra). But when his lawyer misheard the name as "Cadaver" in a cell phone conversation, Jeff knew he had to change the name.

Knowing that online websites were listed in alphabetical order, Jeff wanted a named that began with "A" and he liked the idea that the Amazon River is ten times larger than the next biggest river. He decided on Amazon.com, creating a marketing concept and brand by insisting that the ".com" was a part of the company name.

Laying the Foundation for Amazon.com

Jeff attended a four-day introductory course in bookselling, which sparked his commitment to make customer service *"the cornerstone of Amazon.com,"* by giving the customer an unparalleled shopping experience.

Jeff teamed up with a software engineer who had weathered a few start-up companies and a programmer who wanted to be a part of Jeff's vision. Together, they set up shop in a converted garage and focused their energies on programming the company's infrastructure, including the look of the website, the database that would store customer orders, and an e-mail system to communicate with customers.

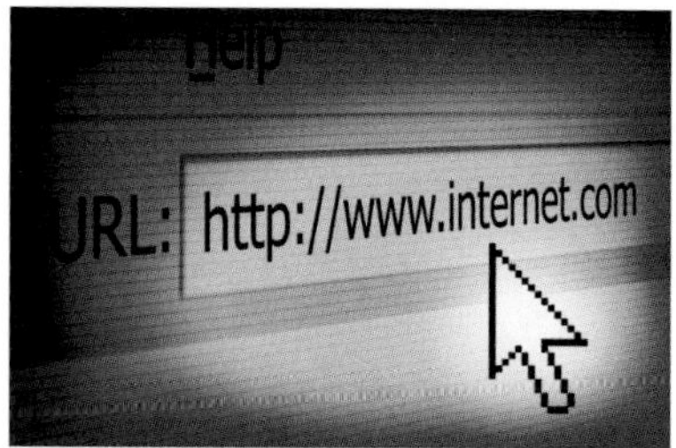

In the spring of 1995, Jeff and his other team members, which by now had grown to five employees, began beta-testing the website. With extension cords running out to the garage to power the company's hardware, the lone circuit breaker wasn't up to handling the load. Running a hair dryer or vacuuming inside the house would blow the circuit breaker.

That's when Jeff moved Amazon.com to a 1,100-square-foot office, with access to a 400-square-foot warehouse, with nothing more than some shelves, a couple of tables with packing supplies, a metered scale and a Pitney Bowes machine.

Amazon.com Takes Off

While Jeff was incredibly optimistic about his company, he conceded that, *"We had very low expectations for starting off, and thought it would take a long, long time for consumer habit to adopt to buying online at all."*

The first week Amazon.com was in business, the company took in $12,438 in sales. During the first month online, Amazon.com shipped orders to 45 countries and all 50 states.

"Our business plan does not even begin to resemble what has actually happened. I think one thing we missed was that the Internet was exclusively made up of early adopters at that time. So all the people online, even though it was a relatively small number compared with today, were those who liked to try new things."

Customers were responding to a number of elements which Amazon.com featured that were unheard of at the time—one-click shopping, customer and staff book reviews, and e-mail order notification.

Sales Skyrocket

Amazon.com wasn't prepared for the major sales volume. *"No one had been hired to do any packing. We were trying to figure how we were going to get enough bandwidth to actually hire more people to do this. We were literally working until midnight every night shipping out 100, 200, 300 packages a day. So everybody pitched in."*

Despite increasing sales, Jeff came close to running out of money to fund his newly launched company. Jeff knew he needed to make the case for Amazon.com with potential investors, stressing that the bookselling site he created on the Internet couldn't exist any other way.

Jeff secured financing and focused on his goal of *"getting big fast."* Within four years, Amazon.com went from zero to more than $2.6 billion in sales and from four people in a renovated garage to a 160,000-square-foot space. Amazon.com revolutionized e-business and changed the way people bought books. Today, the company has a brand that is one of the most familiar in the world.

Kemmons Wilson Builds a New Kind of Motel Experience

It was a vacation that eventually changed lodging around the world—a 1951 cross-country family trip to Washington D.C. that inspired Kemmons Wilson to build the Holiday Inn motel chain. Traveling with his wife, Dorothy, and their five children, Kemmons became frustrated with the second-rate motels he found along the way and the $2 per child surcharge that was prevalent at the time.

Holiday Inn . . .
a brand name you can trust.

A Brand Name Travelers Can Trust

On that vacation, Kemmons told Dorothy he was going to build 400 motels across the country, giving families *"a brand name they could trust"* anywhere they traveled. She was skeptical, but 11 years later, Kemmons fulfilled that promise. He described the inspiration for his new motel chain and Dorothy's skepticism in his autobiography, *Half Luck and Half Brains: The Kemmons Wilson Holiday Inn Story* by Kemmons Wilson, with Robert Kerr.

"The average person just can't afford a vacation, especially with a big family ... I'm going to go home and build a chain of motels that will never charge for children as long as they stay in the same room as their parents."

> *"I don't do a lot of wishful thinking. I'm a dreamer, but I'm a practical dreamer."*
>
> *— Kemmons Wilson*

Kemmons took Dorothy's skepticism in stride. *"She laughed at me, and that's what made me mad and made me do it, I think. I don't do a lot of wishful thinking. I'm a dreamer, but I'm a practical dreamer."*

A Young Entrepreneur

In fact, Kemmons' entrepreneurial spirit was evident early in life. His father died when Kemmons was just an infant and his mother, Doll Wilson, struggled to make ends meet. When she lost her job at the start of the Great Depression, Kemmons decided to quit school and go to work. It didn't take him long for the entrepreneurial "bug" to bite.

Kemmons' love of the movies prompted his first entrepreneurial venture. Realizing that the theater offered no snacks, he bought his first popcorn machine on credit, *"setting a pattern for a lifetime of deals."* His profits soon exceeded the theater manager's income.

The young entrepreneur expanded his business interests to cigarette and pinball machines, movie theaters and jukebox sales, among others. But, it was his foray into home building that would become a cornerstone of his business ventures. Kemmons described a formula he used to finance almost any deal, no matter what its size.

"With enough debt leverage, you could make every dollar work like 10. Leverage is everything, and you can only make money if you use other people's money. You never have to be afraid to go into debt."

Building a New Kind of Motel

Kemmons started buying lots and building houses, using a lumber yard he purchased so he could buy all the materials wholesale. It wasn't until that family trip to Washington D.C. that Kemmons began to formulate his plan to build a new type of motel, with all the comforts and conveniences he and his family found lacking in lodging of the day. He reasoned that satisfied children would mean satisfied parents so he wanted his hotels to have a swimming pool, free ice, air-conditioning in every room, parking near the room, a restaurant on the premises, high cleanliness standards and a rate by the room, not by the number of people in it.

For the rest of the vacation trip, Kemmons used the tape measure he always carried with him to measure every room where he and his family stayed. When the family returned home to Memphis, Kemmons took his sketches to draftsman Eddie Bluestein, who is credited with naming the new motel venture.

While working on Kemmons' plans, Eddie happened to be watching the Bing Crosby movie "Holiday Inn" and jotted the name on the plans. Kemmons liked it… and the name of the new motel chain was decided.

Securing Creative Financing

Kemmons decided to build the first Holiday Inn Hotel Courts in front of his lumberyard on Highway 70, the main route into Memphis from the east. The motel was three times larger than any in the area at the time. A Memphis loan broker helped Kemmons secure financing by negotiating with the owner of a Texas insurance company who agreed to loan Kemmons $325,000 when the hotel was completed.

"With that commitment, I went to the First Tennessee Bank to borrow $325,000 … This was the first loan of that size I did that way. When I built houses, I borrowed money, but I always had the money to pay it off as soon as I sold the house. But, at that point, the loan to build the first Holiday Inn was by far the biggest single loan I had ever had."

A New Era in Travel Begins

The 120-room motel opened in 1952, $45,000 under budget, and complete with its trademark 55-foot sign which forms a giant arrow directing travelers right into the motel.

The timing was just right for Holiday Inn's launch. Construction on a new interstate highway system would soon be underway and more Americans would be taking to the roads. Kemmons was convinced that the *"motel business was the greatest untouched industry in America."*

Launch of One of the First Franchises

Getting to Kemmons' original goal of 400 motels would take some doing. To make Holiday Inn the biggest motel chain in the world, Kemmons asked Wallace Johnson, who was owner of his own successful construction operation, to become his partner. Wallace had a similar background to Kemmons and was vice president of the National Home

Builders Association. Kemmons saw that as a way to take his Holiday Inn motel chain national.

"I realized I had made a big mistake in telling my wife I could build 400 Holiday Inns. Then it dawned on me, if I could get all the big home builders that were members of the Home Builders Association to build one in their home town, I could get 400 real quick."

Wallace agreed and the plan was to get hundreds of hotels in operation quickly and then introduce a national reservation system and marketing program. By selling home builders the plans and license to build Holiday Inns, Kemmons and Wallace launched one of the first business franchise systems in America.

"I didn't know what the word franchising meant, but I needed money."

However, only three of the builders who attended their initial meeting actually followed through and put up a Holiday Inn. Kemmons and Wallace gave up on the home builders and instead found people with capital who wanted to invest, talking them into buying franchises.

"We helped people to build the Inns, and in some cases we built the Inns for them. I worked as much at night as I did in the daytime. I'd go till 11 or 12 at night if there was anybody to tell about Holiday Inn."

KEMMONS WILSON'S BIG IDEA?
Create a motel that caters to the average family.

Kemmons Reaches His 400th Holiday Inn

The company went public in 1957 and by 1962, Kemmons opened his 400th Holiday Inn in Vincennes, Indiana.

"That was probably one of the biggest kicks I ever got, to tell Dorothy about that 400th Holiday Inn."

When Kemmons retired from Holiday Inn 28 years later, there were 1,759 Holiday Inns in 50 different countries. In recounting his success, Kemmons refers back to his original Big Idea.

The Hardest Step Is Coming Up With the Idea

"Sometimes, the first step is the hardest—coming up with an idea. Getting an idea should be like sitting on a pin. It should make you jump up and do something. I've had a great many ideas in my life. And some were good, some were great, and some I'd prefer to forget about."

"The important thing is to take your idea and see it through. Not all of your ideas are going to be good ones. But just remember, 'A man who wins may have been counted out several times, but he didn't hear the referee.'"

Enriching
Women's Lives
In 2008, sales of Mary Kay products
reached $2.6 billion in wholesale sales.

Mary Kay Ash didn't just build a cosmetics company

Mary Kay Cosmetics gives women opportunities

Beginning with an initial investment of $5,000 and a dream of creating a company based on the "Golden Rule," Mary Kay Ash built a cosmetics company that is now a multi-billion dollar business with more than 1.7 million independent sales force members worldwide. It all began with an idea, an indomitable spirit and a "can-do" attitude.

You Can Do It!

When Mary Kay's father was stricken with tuberculosis, her mother became the sole support of the family, leaving seven-year-old Mary Kay to shop for and make the family dinner. Talking her daughter through dinner preparation by phone, Mary Kay's mother always told her, "Honey, you can do it." The phrase stuck with Mary Kay, providing a confidence that she would later call upon in launching her business.

She got married at 17, but at a low point in her life, Mary Kay's marriage dissolved, leaving her to support her three children. She chose a job with flexible hours, as a dealer for Stanley Home Products. She achieved success, sometimes hosting three Stanley parties in one day. After 25 years of direct sales, Mary Kay retired and decided to write her memoirs —a book that would help women overcome some of the obstacles she had encountered, as she describes in her autobiography, *Mary Kay*.

A Company Based on the "Golden Rule"

"First, I wrote down all of the good things the companies I had been with had done and then the changes I would make to create a company that was based on the Golden Rule. I began to dream of a company that would give women the opportunity to do anything in the world they were smart

enough to do. I realized that I didn't have to just sit and wish—I could start that dream company because I had already discovered the ideal product. The skin care products that I loved and had been using faithfully for years would be perfect for my dream company."

Mary Kay bought the formulation for the skin products she loved, developed the strategy and philosophy for her dream company and invested her life savings in it. She approached her business in a different way, eliminating assigned territories and creating a commission structure that was unheard of for a company its size. But, everyone did not rally around her idea.

> *"There's no way, Mary Kay. You can't pay this many cents out of a dollar and still operate."*
>
> *— Mary Kay's accountant*

"When I began Mary Kay, my accountant looked at my proposed commission structure and said, 'There's no way, Mary Kay. You can't pay this many cents out of a dollar and still operate.' My accountant was not the only disbeliever when I began talking about my dream. Many well-intentioned people, including my attorney, assured me it would fail. After all, who ever heard of a company based on the Golden Rule?"

Mary Kay persevered with her business idea. She had remarried by this point in her life and she and her husband decided that he would run the administrative end of the business while she focused on what she knew best—sales.

"My dream company was about to become a reality. When a man starts a business, he usually establishes monetary goals, such as 'We're going to do a hundred thousand dollars the first year.' I'm often asked what my financial objectives were when we first started Mary Kay Cosmetics. Well, I didn't have any. My interest was in offering women opportunities that in 1963 didn't exist anywhere else."

Persevering Despite Tragedy

A month before the company was to open its doors, her dream faced another huge setback—with very personal consequences. Mary Kay's husband suffered a fatal heart attack.

"The company was my dream and my idea, but I had never planned to run it alone. I knew I didn't have the skills or experience for the administrative end. And yet, all the merchandise and bottles and labels were useless if the company folded. I had to go on."

Mary Kay turned to her attorney and accountant for their advice. They both counseled her to liquidate the business. "Recoup whatever cash you can," said her attorney. "If you don't, you'll end up penniless."

MARY KAY'S BIG IDEA?

Offer women opportunities that don't exist anywhere else.

Her Family Rallies to Her Support

After her husband's funeral, Mary Kay's two sons and her daughter rallied to her support, repeating back to her what she had told them all their lives, "You can do it!"

Mary Kay's son, Richard Rogers, gave up a promising career and took a salary cut to help her run the business and her other children joined her later. *"We've watched you all our lives make a success of everything you've done. If you could be successful working for someone else, we know you can do even better working for yourself,"* said Richard, who was 20 years old at the time.

Mary Kay launched her business in 1963—exactly one month to the day after her husband passed away. The first headquarters was in a 500-square-foot storefront in Dallas, with used furniture, homemade drapes and a single metal shelf from Sears.

But Mary Kay was excited about their business location since it was occupied by 5,000 women who worked in different offices.

Creatively Attracting Customers

"We figured we'd get lots of sales from that captive market. But in the morning, they were rushing to get to work on time, and in the evening, they were anxious to get home. The only advantage we had was that they did get coffee breaks twice a day. Before very long, we learned to give the fastest facials you've ever seen!"

Mary Kay and her family also offered wigs and a wig stylist to help draw customers in to learn about her unknown line of cosmetics. She and her sons would put in 16- and 18-hour workdays when they first started the business. But the hard work paid off.

Mary Kay's Legacy

Mary Kay's independent sales force thrived in the recognition-based environment she created ... and the opportunities that she provided to women remain her legacy.

> *"The success [of Mary Kay Inc.] is much, much deeper than just dollars and cents and buildings and assets. The real success of our Company is measured to me in the lives that have been touched and given hope."*

Pierre Omidyar Connects Buyers and Sellers Via the Internet

BID SELL

eBay levels the playing field with online auction

Born in Paris in 1967, Pierre Omidyar was a self-professed "geek" who enjoyed taking apart gadgets as a kid. It was his passion for computers that led him to launch a website that revolutionized the way people buy and sell all across the world ... eBay.

Pierre moved to the United States when he was six years old and his first exposure to computers was in grade school. He would cut gym class to go play on a Radio Shack TRS-80 computer with 4K of memory. It wasn't until high school that he got his first paying computer job—writing a program to print library catalogue cards for $6 an hour.

Pursue Your Passion

Pierre's first choice was to major in computer engineering at Tufts University. He found the curriculum a bit too rigorous and switched to computer science, teaching himself how to program the Macintosh. He shared his motivation in an Academy of Achievement interview in 2000:

> **"I was just pursuing what I enjoyed doing. And the ability to create software that could have a benefit or an impact on people that used it was what was driving me. And like most software people, it is very much a passion more than anything else. And so, like people have said, it is not really work, you know, if you are having fun, it's not work so that was the case with me."**

Launching a Company before eBay

After college, Pierre worked at an Apple subsidiary called Claris and later formed a company called Ink Development Corporation with several colleagues. The company's main focus was developing software that would enable people to operate computers using a pen stylus instead of a keyboard and mouse. It was a side project, which involved creating software to manage online shopping, that took off. Pierre left the company to take a new position as a software engineer at General Magic, an Apple offshoot, but he retained a controlling interest in his company. The Ink Development Corporation was renamed eShop and later sold to Microsoft, making Pierre a millionaire.

It was while he was at General Magic, that Pierre began to tinker on his time off, writing code for an online auction site that would let everyday people do business with each other on the Internet. He launched the bare-bones site on Labor Day weekend 1995 calling it AuctionWeb.

Leveling the Playing Field

"I wanted to create an efficient market where individuals could benefit, kind of level the playing field. And I thought, 'Gee, the Internet, the web, it's perfect for this.' This is more of an intellectual pursuit, you know, than anything else. It was just an idea that I had, and I started it as an

experiment, as a side hobby basically, while I had my day job. And it just kind of grew. Within six months, it was earning revenue that was paying my costs. Within nine months, the revenue was more than I was making on my day job, and that's kind of when the light bulb went off. 'Knock, knock, knock. You've got a business here, do something about it.'"

A Belief in People's Honesty

In addition to leveling the playing field for commerce, Pierre structured his site using his basic belief in people's honesty as the tenet. A year after the site's launch, he proposed his idea of a Feedback Forum, a place online where both buyers and sellers could rate each other and give feedback on how their transactions were conducted.

"I founded the company on the notion that people were basically good, and that if you give them the benefit of the doubt you're rarely disappointed. And I'm thankful that, in fact, statistics have borne that out to be true. And it is actually: 99.999 percent of our transactions happen without a case of reported fraud."

One of the first items sold on AuctionWeb was a broken laser pointer that Pierre owned. It sold for

$14. What began as way to buy and sell computer and electronics equipment, Beanie Babies and other collectibles began to sky-rocket and expand. Today, eBay users worldwide trade more than $1,900 worth of goods on the site every second.

Individuals Take Back the Power of the Market

In 1997, Pierre changed the name of his site to eBay. He liked the name EchoBay, but the domain name was already taken, so he shortened it to eBay instead. Users of the new auction site are active community members, even to the point of creating the features of the website itself as Pierre described in a 2001 *BusinessWeek* article:

"I wanted to give the power of the market back to individuals, not just large corporations," says Omidyar. *"It was letting the users take responsibility for building the community—even the building of the Web site."*

> **"I WANTED TO GIVE THE POWER OF THE MARKET BACK TO INDIVIDUALS, NOT JUST LARGE CORPORATIONS."**
>
> — *Pierre Omidyar*

"Pierre answered e-mails from eBay's users during the day and at night he rewrote the site's software to incorporate their suggestions, from fixing software bugs to creating new product categories," BusinessWeek reported.

Rapid Growth, but Also Setbacks

For the first two years of eBay's existence, the company grew at 20 to 30 percent every single month. But that kind of growth also caused the company to lag in its infrastructure. In fact, a fairly public failure occurred for eBay in mid-1999, when systems went down for 22 hours and then eight hours after that. The event was front page news and after that, Pierre brought on Meg Whitman as CEO to focus on infrastructure and technology.

"And I think failure of that magnitude, or a challenge of that magnitude is really important and I'm glad that we faced it so early in our evolution. They say, 'If it doesn't kill you, it makes you stronger,' and it's true. And what you learn from those challenges and those failures are what will get you past the next ones."

Today, what started as Pierre's hobby is now the world's largest online marketplace—where practically anyone can sell practically anything at any time. With a presence in 39 markets, including the U.S., and approximately 88 million active users worldwide, eBay has changed the face of Internet commerce. It all began with Pierre's idea to offer a way for people to connect with each other and create a level playing field for trade over the Internet.

Believe in What You're Doing

"You should pursue your passion. If you're passionate about something and you work hard, then I think you'll be successful. If you start a business because you think you're going to make a lot of money at it, then you probably won't be successful, because that's the wrong reason to start a business. You have to really believe in what you're doing, be passionate enough about it so that you will put in the hours and hard work that it takes to actually succeed there, and then you'll be successful.

"So just go and do it, try it, learn from it. You'll fail at some things, that's a learning experience that you need so that you can take that on to the next experience. And don't let people who you may respect and who you believe know what they're talking about, don't let them tell you it can't be done, because often they will tell you it can't be done, and it's just because they don't have the courage to try."

Ray Kroc Creates the Ultimate Franchise

★ ★ ★ ★ ★

McDonald's stresses a uniform method of preparation

Today, McDonald's is as American as, well... hamburgers. It wasn't until 1954, that a 52-year-old Ray Kroc had the vision to expand and standardize a chain of restaurants Americans could depend on for consistent quality in their hamburgers, fries and milkshakes, no matter where they traveled. Ray's idea transformed the restaurant franchise business and made McDonald's the largest fast-food chain in the world.

Ray didn't always have his sights set on creating a restaurant empire. He began his career playing piano, but soon found his calling as a paper cup salesman for the Lily Tulip Cup Co. As his customer base grew, Ray met Earl Prince, owner of Prince Castle, who had invented the Multimixer, a six-spindle machine that made big volume milkshake production possible.

Striking Out On His Own

Earl suggested that Ray become the exclusive distributor for the Multimixer in the country. After mortgaging his home to fund gaining exclusive rights to the product as president of his own company—Prince Castle Sales—Ray did just that. His young wife, Ethel, was not pleased that Ray gave up his secure position selling paper cups. In his autobiography, *Grinding It Out: The Making of McDonald's,* with Robert Anderson, Ray recalls his wife's reaction:

"You just have to trust my instincts. I am positive this is going to be a winner."

— Ray Kroc

"You're risking your whole future if you do this, Ray," she said. "You are thirty-five years old, and you are going to start all over again as if you were twenty? This Multimixer seems good now, but what if it turns out to be just a fad and fails?"

"You just have to trust my instincts," I told her. *"I'm positive this is going to be a winner."*

An Idea Takes Shape

Ray did successfully sell the Multimixer for more than 15 years, but he knew he needed to find a new market. Ray began to hear stories about a restaurant run by the McDonald brothers in San Bernardino, California, *"who kept eight Multimixers whirring up a bucket brigade of milkshakes."*

At the pristine California restaurant, Maurice and Richard McDonald had a menu stripped down to the minimum, but it was the quality, price and efficiency of the operation that kept customers coming back every day.

> *"Hamburgers, fries and beverages were prepared on an assembly line basis. Of course, the simplicity of the procedure allowed the McDonalds to concentrate on quality in every step, and that was the trick. When I saw it working that day in 1954, I felt like some latter-day Newton who'd just had an Idaho potato caromed off his skull."*

In his hotel room that night, Ray reflected on what he had seen and an idea began to take shape. *"Visions of McDonald's restaurants dotting crossroads all over the country paraded through my brain. In each store, of course, were eight Multimixers whirring away and paddling a steady flow of cash into my pockets."*

Getting a National Franchise Off the Ground

Ray decided to pitch the idea of opening several restaurants across the country, using their design and operation, to the McDonald brothers. While the McDonald brothers had sold some franchises in the area, they didn't want to launch a broader chain of restaurants.

"It'll be a lot of trouble," Dick McDonald objected. *"Who could we get to open them for us?"*

"Well," Ray answered, *"What about me?"*

So, Ray drew up an agreement with the McDonald brothers to franchise copies of their operation across the United States. The franchises would retain the signature arches the San Bernardino McDonald's had going right through its roof, as well as the McDonald's name and menu.

Reception to Ray's new business venture was cool. His wife, his former secretary and his golfing buddies thought he had lost his mind. But Ray plunged in and began looking for a location for his first McDonald's restaurant.

"I needed to get a location that I could establish as a model for others to follow. My plan was to oversee it in my spare time from the Prince Castle business."

He found just the right location in Des Plaines, Illinois, 17 miles from his home, and after hiring a close friend's son-in-law to manage it, Ray opened his first McDonald's on April 15, 1955.

Overcoming the Great French Fry Flop

But there were problems right from the beginning, from having to include a furnace in the new location that could withstand Chicago-area winters, (something not included in the McDonald brothers' plans for a slab location in a semi-desert climate), to what Ray called the *"great french fry flop."*

He instructed his new store manager to prepare the fries in exactly the same manner he had seen at the McDonald's restaurant in San Bernardino. But the results were disappointing. Instead of crispy, delicious fries, the method produced bland, mushy ones.

"This was a tremendously frustrating situation. My whole idea de-

McDonald's
KROC'S SECRET FORMULA?
Emphasize the importance of details.
You must perfect every fundamental of your business
if you expect it to perform well.

pended on carrying out the McDonald's standard of taste and quality in hundreds of stores, and here I couldn't even do it in the first one!"

With the help of experts at the Potato and Onion Association, Ray learned that, without their knowledge, the natural desert air in the McDonald brothers' open bins had helped to cure the potatoes. So Ray added an electric fan to provide a continuous burst of air on the potatoes in Ray's new store, prompting his manager to tell him that they *"had the most pampered potatoes."*

That first store began to make a profit. Three other stores quickly followed and by 1960, there were more than 200 McDonald's across the country.

Quality, Service, Cleanliness and Value

Ray stressed QSC & V (Quality, Service, Cleanliness and Value) in all of his stores as a way to ensure a consistent customer experience. But, it was a decision to make the company's business—developing restaurants and getting franchises to operate them—that set the stage for McDonald's rapid growth.

"We wanted McDonald's to be more than just a name used by many different people. We wanted to build a restaurant system that would be

known for food of consistently high quality and uniform methods of preparation. Our aim, of course, was to insure repeat business based on the system's reputation rather than on the quality of a single store or operator."

But, as his fast-food business began to grow, Ray continued to have legal issues with the McDonald brothers, having written the initial agreement by himself.

"There's an old saying that a man who represents himself has a fool for a lawyer, and it certainly applied in this instance. I was just carried away by the thought of McDonald's drive-ins proliferating like rabbits, with eight Multimixers in each one."

So in 1961, with a loan arranged by a New York money manager, Ray was able to buy out the McDonald brothers for $2.7 million.

As McDonald's continued to expand, Ray treated his franchisees as business partners and hired people on his management team who mirrored his persistence and determination to make the business a success.

"Once in a while I have had great ideas strike me in the middle of the

night—sweeping plans that I could see complete, or so it seemed. But, every time, these things turned out in the clear light of the following day to be more fanciful than functional. And the reason usually was that some small but essential detail had been overlooked in my grand design. So, at the risk of seeming simplistic, I emphasize the importance of details. You must perfect every fundamental of your business if you expect it to perform well.

"People have marveled at the fact that I didn't start McDonald's until I was fifty-two years old and then I became a success overnight. But I was just like a lot of show business personalities who work away quietly at their craft for years, and then, suddenly, they get the right break and make it big. I was an overnight success, all right, but thirty years is a long, long night."

Roxanne Quimby's Informal Focus Groups Lead to Marketing Success

Burt's Bees expands product line

It was a partnership formed alongside a country road. That's where Roxanne Quimby first met Burt Shavitz, a reclusive beekeeper who sold honey in gallon jars at a roadside stand. Their meeting led to the launch of Burt's Bees, an entrepreneurial story that breaks the mold, just like the two backwoods pioneers who started the company with no capital, or even electricity!

In 1984, Roxanne, a divorced mother of two, stopped to buy some honey on the way to her waitress job. She and her children were living in a cabin without electricity and she washed her children's diapers in water heated on a wood stove—choosing this way of life because she didn't want to compromise. When Roxanne saw Burt's honey, she also saw a business opportunity … and a way for her to provide more opportunities for her children.

"I fell back on what I could do—making and selling handmade arts & crafts at local and regional outdoor shows."

— Roxanne Quimby

A Business Opportunity for Her Future

"I was living in a very remote area in Maine at the time where there were few 'real' jobs for an unskilled art school graduate like me," Roxanne told *Hilary Magazine's* Heather Riccio and Hilary Rowland. *"So I fell back on what I could do—making and selling handmade arts & crafts at local and regional outdoor shows. This way of earning a living also gave me the flexibility I needed to raise my children."*

Roxanne teamed up with Burt, handling the business end of their venture. First, she traded the large gallon jars Burt had been using for his honey for small beehive-shaped jars with handmade labels. Then she started making candles from the beeswax Burt had stored, later experimenting on her wood stove with other products made from the beeswax, including stove and shoe polish. The two began selling their all-natural products at craft fairs in New England, bringing in $200 at their very first fair.

Paying Attention to Detail

In an *INC Magazine* interview in 2004 with Susan Donovan, Roxanne described her approach to market research:

"At the fairs, I focused closely on what sold the most and tried to figure out why. I didn't know it then, but it was like having one focus group after another. I learned, for instance, that when people pick up a candle, they turn it over. For some reason they want to see the bottom, so I made sure the candles were nicely finished with a sharp knife to smooth the mold."

As sales began to increase, they moved their operations from Roxanne's cabin to a one-room schoolhouse they rented for $150 a year. The space was right, even though it also had no heat, electricity, running water or windows. Roxanne's goal was to make $10,000, but by the end of their first year in business, sales were already double that.

The Business Gets a Boost

In a 2000 *Fortune Magazine* interview with Julie Sloane, Roxanne described a break they got from a trendy New York boutique:

"Zona is a trend-setting boutique in New York City that was so innovative people would line up to get in the store. In the early 1990s the owner saw our teddy bear candles at a crafts fair and bought a couple dozen. They sold so well that every week he would call and order another 200. Buyers from the big retail stores and catalogs would stop in to see what was hot at Zona. That's how we got some great customers: Gardener's Eden, Smith & Hawken, Smithsonian Museum Store. I never called stores cold and pitched my products. They would come to us at the trade shows. Our sales doubled every year."

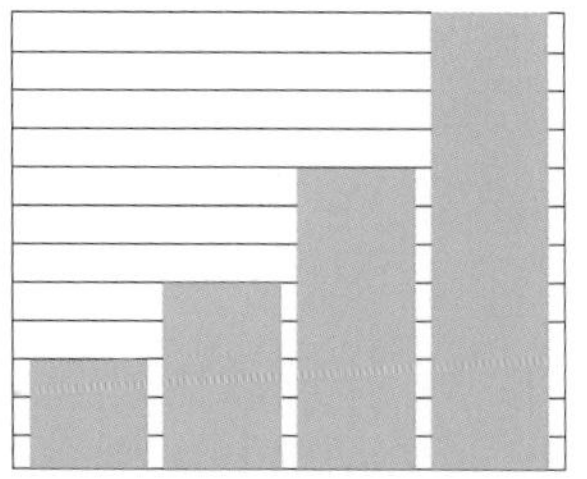

To accommodate the increasing orders, Roxanne moved the business to an abandoned bowling alley and hired 40 employees. The company incorporated in 1991 and was making half a million candles a year, as well as natural soaps and perfumes still cooked up on gas stoves. That was also the year Burt's Bees added lip balm to their product line, which remains their best-selling product to this day.

A Move Puts the Business in Survival Mode

With products and sales expanding to $3 million by 1993, Roxanne knew the business needed to move to a new location that was less expensive than Maine. She chose North Carolina—an area that was home to some internationally known personal care products companies.

"But the move was badly planned and poorly organized," Roxanne told *Fortune*. *"We just loaded our stuff into nine vans and drove south. We had to stop shipping for six weeks. That cut off our cash flow. As a result, we were fighting for survival that year. I cut half the product line right away. I took a million and a half dollars in business and discontinued it. All the handmade stuff was eliminated—the candles, the honey, the organic cotton baby clothes. I kept the products whose production could be automated, the lip balms and moisturizing creams. We'd been doing everything by hand, and that was pretty primitive. Now we're fully automated."*

Roxanne also took the opportunity to hire managers from the local cosmetic companies with experience in manufacturing, shipping, marketing, and finance. She eventually bought Burt out of his share of the company when he retired, and sold 80 percent of the company to a private-equity firm in 2003.

Today, Burt's Bees is the leading manufacturer of Earth-friendly natural personal care products. In her *Hilary Magazine* interview, Roxanne attributes the success of the business to old-fashioned values:

"I think it takes a lot of hard work, persistence, and belief in one's vision to build a successful company. That sounds sort of trite but one must possess these basic traits to carry on when faced with the daily challenges and sheer exhaustion of running one's own company. Good luck and good timing also play a role in one's success. For a product-driven company like Burt's Bees, I think it's important to stay ahead of the curve with product innovation and listen closely to what the consumer tells you she wants, and remain faithful to your mission and values.

"No matter how trite it sounds, one must be faithful to one's vision and not settle for less no matter what the odds. Building a business requires a lot of personal and financial sacrifices that were unknown to me when I started out. Would I do it again? Absolutely!"

"... listen closely to what the consumer tells you she wants, and remain faithful to your mission and values."

— ROXANNE QUIMBY

Sam Walton Saw Opportunity in Small Town America

Walmart perfects the art of discounting

★ ★ ★ ★ ★

The founder of the world's largest retailer, Sam Walton, started small, by selling magazine subscriptions when he was seven years old. He held a paper route from the time he was in the seventh grade all the way through college, where he balanced that with waiting tables and being a lifeguard. Graduating with a business degree from the University of Missouri, Sam contemplated going on to Wharton School of Finance, but couldn't afford it, so he accepted a job as a management trainee at J.C. Penney.

"Now I realize the simple truth. I got into retailing because I was tired and I wanted a real job," he said in his autobiography, *Sam Walton: Made in America*, with John Huey. *"Maybe I was born to be a merchant. I know this for sure. I loved retail from the very beginning."*

Sam's first foray into retailing on his own was his purchase of a Ben Franklin store franchise in Newport, Arkansas, funded with his own money as well as money from his father-in-law.

It Didn't Take Long to Start Experimenting

"At the very beginning, I went along and ran my store by their book because I really didn't know any better. But it didn't take me long to start experimenting. Pretty soon I was laying on promotion programs of my own and I started buying merchandise directly from manufacturers. That was the start of the practices that prevail at Walmart today."

In his experimentation, he learned a simple lesson about discounting that would eventually change the way retailers sell and customers buy across America. "**This is really the essence of discounting—by cutting your price, you can boost your sales to a point where you earn far more at the cheaper retail price than you would have by selling the item at the higher price.**"

A legal error forced him to give up his first store. *"I had neglected to include a clause in my lease which gave me an option to renew after the first five years. It was the low point of my business life. I had built the best variety store in the whole region and worked hard in the community—done everything right—and now I was being kicked out of town. But, I've always thought of problems as challenges and I read my leases a lot more carefully after that."*

A Strategy Instrumental to Walmart's Success

Sam's wife, Helen, refused to move to any town with more than 10,000 people—a small town emphasis that was later instrumental in Walmart's success. So Sam found an old variety store to buy in Bentonville, Arkansas, a town of 3,000 people and started over. Although it was another Ben Franklin franchise, Sam called the store Walton's Five and Dime and set it up as a self-service store with the checkout registers

> *"Somehow over the years, folks have gotten the impression that Walmart was something I dreamed up out of the blue as a middle-aged man. It's true that I was forty-four when we opened our first Walmart in 1962."*
>
> *— Sam Walton*

in front—a new concept at the time, which was used in only two other stores.

Sam began to buy variety stores and learned that by building larger stores, he could do unheard of amounts of business for variety stores, unthinkable for small towns. After researching early discounters, he knew that discounting was the future of retailing. He approached Butler Brothers, the regional retailer that operated the Ben Franklin stores, about backing him in his discounting venture, but they turned him down. Sam realized he had to strike out on his own, even though it meant leaving the franchise discount store business and building his own distribution system.

The 1st Walmart—Just Another Experiment

"Somehow over the years, folks have gotten the impression that Walmart was something I dreamed up out of the blue as a middle-aged man. It's true that I was forty-four when we opened our first Walmart in 1962, but

the store was really an outgrowth of everything we'd been doing since Newport-another case of me being unable to leave well enough alone, another experiment. And like most other overnight successes, it was about 20 years in the making. Nobody wanted to gamble on

that first Walmart. Helen and I pledged houses and property, everything we had. Most folks, including my own brother, Bud, were pretty skeptical of the whole concept. They thought Walmart was just another one of Sam Walton's crazy ideas. It was totally unproven at the time, but it was really what we were doing all along: experimenting, trying to do something different, educating ourselves as to what was going on in the retail industry and trying to stay ahead of those trends."

Using the principles of discounting and promotion that Sam Walton experimented with in his early years of retailing, Walmart has grown to be the world's largest retailer, with more than 8,000 retail units in 15 countries. Sam attributed much of his success to what he termed *"swimming upstream."*

The Best Opportunities Are Created Out of Necessity

"Many of our best opportunities were created out of necessity. The things that we were forced to learn and do, because we started out under-financed and under-capitalized in these remote, small communities contributed mightily to the way we've grown as a company. Had we been capitalized, or had we been the offshoot of a large corporation the way I wanted to be, we might not ever have tried all the small towns we were into in the early days. It turned out that the first lesson we learned was that there was much, much more business out there in small-town America than anybody, including me, had ever dreamed of."

SAM'S BIG IDEA?

By discounting you can boost sales—

to a point where you earn far more at the cheaper retail price than you would have by selling the item at the higher price.

Sara Blakely Eliminates the Lines

Spanx gets the "thumbs up" from a mill owner

If Sara Blakely's first career aspiration had been successful, her company, Spanx, might never have been launched. Sara had hoped to be a trial attorney. When she failed the LSAT, she turned to other career endeavors, including selling fax machines and office copiers, and even a fledgling career as a stand-up comedienne.

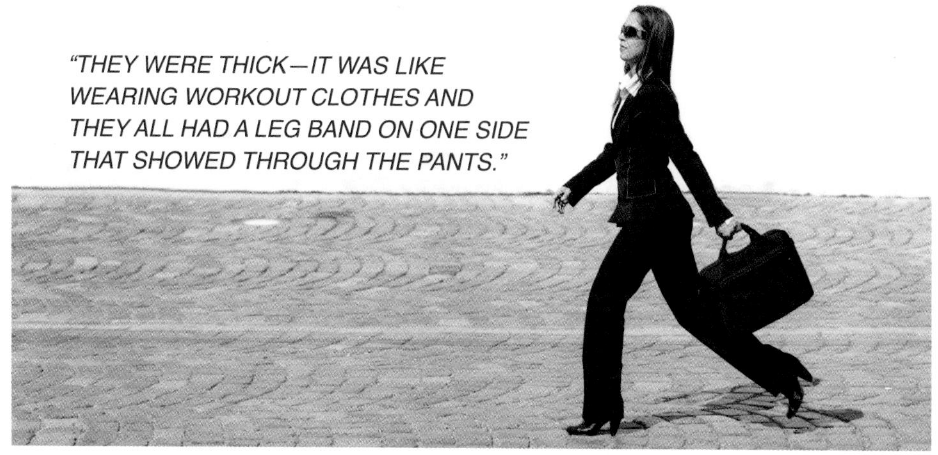

But, it wasn't until she struggled to find a solution to a vexing appearance dilemma—eliminating unsightly panty lines—that she had the Big Idea for Spanx. She described her moment of inspiration to *BusinessWeek.com* reporter Stacy Perman in a 2007 interview:

"I did not like the way I looked in a pair of white pants. I was 27 at the time and spent a lot of money on them but you could see panty lines. Nothing worked. I shopped for body shapers for the first time in my life and I was horrified. They were thick—it was like wearing workout clothes and they all had a leg band on one side that showed through the pants. So I cut the feet off of a pair of panty hose and it allowed me to wear a pair of great strappy sandals. I didn't see lines but the hose rolled up at my feet—and that's how Spanx was born."

Overcoming Rejections

Never having taken a business class, Sara researched panty hose patents after work, wrote the patent herself and finally found a lawyer to help her write the claim. She invested $5,000 and drawing upon her cold-calling experience, Sara spent the next two years working nights and weekends out of her apartment to get a prototype made.

Her idea was not an easy sale ... at first. Taking a week off of work, she begged mill owners to help her make her prototype, but many thought her idea "would never sell." She finally found a mill owner who *"decided to help me make my crazy idea,"* but only after he got "a thumbs up" from his daughters who didn't think the idea was crazy at all.

"I was my own focus group. I had already tried the product and I saw what it did for me. I knew if they said 'no', they just didn't get it. I never second-guessed the product. Before it was actually made, I did hear 'no' a lot. It was very discouraging. At times I stopped out of discouragement, but I never lost confidence in the fact that it was a good idea."

With a prototype in hand, Sara began calling on some of the top retail stores in the country, sometimes illustrating the product's benefits herself. For example, modeling her prototype "before and after" under her cream-colored pants was a deciding factor in Neiman Marcus becoming her first retail customer. Three weeks later, Spanx was on the shelves. Using a friend's computer at night after work, Sara had designed the packaging herself which featured a bold, new look, unlike anything on store shelves.

It Hit Me Like a Lightning Bolt

Choosing just the right product name is often a key element of business success:

> *"I knew that Kodak and Coca-Cola are the two most recognized names in the world, and they both have a predominant 'K' sound in them. Also, from doing stand-up comedy, it is a known secret that the 'K' sound makes people laugh. So for good luck, I wanted my product's name to have the 'K' sound in it, and Spanks hit me like a lightning bolt. I immediately knew it was perfect! At the last minute I changed the 'KS' to an 'X' after doing research that made-up words do better for products than real words (and are easier to trademark). Spanx is edgy, fun, extremely catchy, and for a moment it makes your mind wander."*

The Oprah Factor

In her first three months in business, Sara sold over 50,000 pairs of footless panty hose from the back of her apartment and the company has been profitable from the first month. But it wasn't until Spanx was mentioned on the Oprah Winfrey Show that sales really began to skyrocket.

"Oprah had chosen Spanx as one of her favorite products in 2000. I had boxes of product in my apartment and two weeks notice that she was going to say she loved it on TV. I had no shipping department. It was pretty intense and a fabulous call to get as an entrepreneur and it got the ball in motion quickly."

Spanx expanded its distribution to other major department stores including Saks and Nordstrom and Sara moved the company out of her apartment to offices in Decatur, Georgia, in 2001. The next year, she was named "Entrepreneur of the Year" for the Southeast Region by Ernst and Young.

Listen to Your Gut

Since then, Sara has expanded both her product line and the number of retailers who feature her products, including a new line for Target, as well as others in the U.K. Since she first got her Big Idea, Sara attributes the successful launch of Spanx to listening to her gut.

"I think that there is a fine line between ignorance and confidence. I didn't know how to run a business and I had never taken a business course in my life. From the beginning, I had no board of advisors and nobody to consult on this journey except for my own gut. I am a case study of 'if you didn't know how this is done, this is how you do it.' Now I give speeches and I always ask, 'If no one showed you how to do your job, how would you be doing it?' Take a moment and ask that question. Often your way is better. Maybe it's a fresh new approach. If you are doing something the way that everyone is doing it, you are not really creating change by doing it that way.

"Perseverance is the key to starting a successful business. You have to believe in yourself. It's an insane amount of hard work. I don't want to underestimate that for someone who wants to start their own business. I worked 24/7 for at least four years to launch Spanx."

TEN TIPS FOR SUCCESS

There's no one-size fits all for entrepreneurs. Some, like Jeff Bezos, get their Big Ideas for launching a business early in life. Others, like Ray Kroc, feel the pull of the entrepreneurial spirit in the prime of their lives.

Although all Big Ideas are unique, I found that there are some common denominators in turning an idea into reality. They are:

Be Passionate About Your Big Idea

Examine your motives for wanting to launch your business. Successful entrepreneurs don't look first at how full their bank accounts will be if they're able to get their new business off the ground. They want to make a difference in the world through their Big Idea—solving a common problem, offering an easier way to do things, developing a new product that fulfills an unmet niche.

Passion is the underlying thread for success. There's no doubt about it, starting a business is a lot of hard work. It's your passion for your Big Idea that will see you through any obstacles that will come your way.

Just look at eBay's Pierre Omidyar, who followed his passion for computer programming and saw a unique niche that could be filled on the Internet. Writing code for the launch of his online auction site while still working full-time, Pierre was focused on creating software that would benefit people, rather than solely on making money.

"You have to really believe in what you're doing, be passionate enough about it so that you'll put in the hours and hard work that it takes to actually succeed," Pierre said.

Passion—it's the driving force that you just can't ignore. It's what will make your new adventure seem more like fun, than work. It's the difference between wanting to start a business and craving it.

> **"SUCCESS IS NOT THE KEY TO HAPPINESS. HAPPINESS IS THE KEY TO SUCCESS. IF YOU LOVE WHAT YOU ARE DOING, YOU WILL BE SUCCESSFUL."**
>
> — *Albert Schweitzer*

2 Let Quality Differentiate Your Product or Service

Maintain the quality of your product or service. Your product or service is your calling card…and your business reputation. Like Mary Kay, who built her business on the "Golden Rule," you should create the same type of experience for your customers that you would like to receive.

For Kemmons Wilson, his commitment to quality spawned the idea of giving families an alternative to the second-rate motels prevalent during the early 1950s. That alternative standardized amenities travelers now take for granted and differentiated the Holiday Inn motel chain in the travel industry.

With all of the competing interests and expenses a start-up company faces, there may be a temptation to lessen the quality of your product in order to cut costs, but it is your relationship with your customers that will suffer. And that's a relationship that all entrepreneurs cannot afford to damage or take lightly.

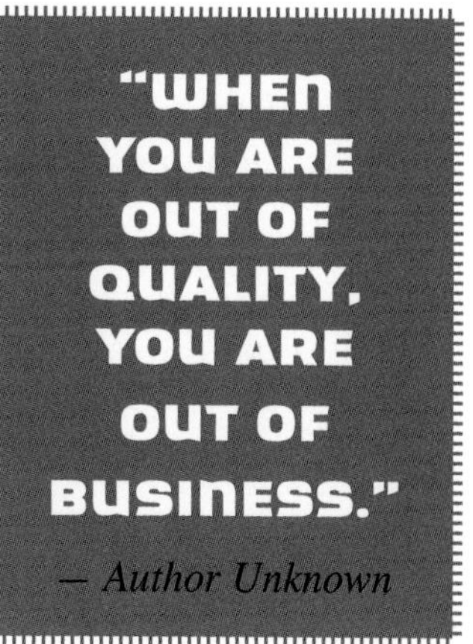

3 Select Your Company Name Carefully

Your company name is your identity, so choose it carefully to best communicate your mission and your brand. From Spanx creator Sara Blakely to Jeff Bezos selecting Amazon.com rather than Cadabra Inc., successful entrepreneurs know that capturing customer attention is a key first step to launching your business.

So take the time to brainstorm and try on the sight, sound and connotations of various names. Choose a name that's short, memorable, has a positive feel to it and as much as possible, one that captures what your business does. Think about how your business name will look on your business logo and if people will remember how to spell it when searching for your website. Be sure to check with the United States Patent and Trademark Office and domain registers to see if your suggested name is available to do business under.

Let your company name make a great first impression for your new business.

> **"HAVE REGARD FOR YOUR NAME, SINCE IT WILL REMAIN FOR YOU LONGER THAN A GREAT STORE OF GOLD."**
>
> – *The Apocrypha, Ecclesiasticus*

Believe In Yourself

As you begin to put your Big Idea into action, there won't be a shortage of naysayers who may think your idea has no merit. To create a business where there was none before, you have to steadfastly believe in the benefits your business idea will bring to others.

In each of the success stories listed in this book, the entrepreneur listened to what others around them had to say, but believed that what each of them felt in his or her gut was right … and then acted on it.

Cookie connoisseur Debbi Fields is a great example of following through on instincts. Everyone around her told her the cookie business would not be a success, even as they devoured her chewy delights. But she knew in her heart that she was on to a great idea … and more importantly, followed through on that idea.

Entrepreneurs see opportunity where others do not. Listen to the concerns of others. (They may have thought of something you haven't.) But, trust your own judgment and believe in your own idea. If you don't, who will?

> "DON'T LIMIT YOURSELF. MANY PEOPLE LIMIT THEMSELVES TO WHAT THEY THINK THEY CAN DO. YOU CAN GO AS FAR AS YOUR MIND LETS YOU. WHAT YOU BELIEVE, REMEMBER, YOU CAN ACHIEVE."
>
> – *Mary Kay Ash*

5 Step Out of Your Comfort Zone

Entrepreneurial is another word for risk. But for successful entrepreneurs, starting a business is a calculated risk, one they investigate thoroughly before taking the leap. It is that leap which differentiates entrepreneurs from would-be business owners. Every entrepreneur with a Big Idea has some trepidation about leaving the security of a salaried income.

Starbucks' Howard Schultz took a huge pay cut to get his "feet wet" initially as Starbucks' head of marketing. But, he really stepped out of his comfort zone in launching his own company, betting that Americans would enjoy espresso served right in stores, as he had during his trip to Italy. He knew that making the decision was a milestone moment—one that would affect the rest of his life, and that of his young family. He also knew that he had to try.

The fear of regret is a powerful motivator for moving beyond any qualms … and taking action. Those with an entrepreneurial spirit don't want to look back on their lives and regret not stepping out of their comfort zones, missing the opportunities that could have changed the course of their lives for the better.

"OFTEN THE DIFFERENCE BETWEEN A SUCCESSFUL PERSON AND A FAILURE IS NOT ONE HAS BETTER ABILITIES OR IDEAS, BUT THE COURAGE THAT ONE HAS TO BET ON ONE'S IDEAS, TO TAKE A CALCULATED RISK – AND TO ACT."

— *Andre Malraux*

6 The "Devil Is in the Details"

Everyone knows that if you eat at a McDonald's in New Jersey or New Mexico, you'll experience the same quality ... thanks to Founder Ray Kroc's commitment to detail. Ray understood that if you focus on the small stuff—the myriad of details it takes to construct a burger in an assembly-line fashion—you'll be rewarded with consistent quality and efficiency.

Regardless of what your product or service is, as an entrepreneur you'll be faced with a long "to-do" list—from developing a business plan, defining your customer niche, securing capital, laying the groundwork for your infrastructure, deciding your marketing plan, building relationships with suppliers, planning cash flow to hiring staff and launching day-to-day operations.

> **"A MAN'S ACCOMPLISHMENTS IN LIFE ARE THE CUMULATIVE EFFECT OF HIS ATTENTION TO DETAIL."**
>
> *– John Foster Dulles*

That "to-do" list is often longer than there are hours in a day. But each element of a business is important and deserves its due because the "devil is in the details."

Take the time to do the research and legwork, reaching out to experts (accountants, lawyers, marketers) for advice, when you need it. The more time you put in up-front, the smoother your transition to owning your own business will be.

7 Experiment and Listen to Your Customers

Landing your first customer is only the first step in making your business successful; you need to continually exceed your customers' expectations to keep them coming back for more.

Outstanding customer service will help differentiate your business from the competition. Respond quickly to customer issues and resolve them with respect. Listening to your customers about what you are doing well and not so well provides an opportunity to fine tune products and processes or to uncover additional customer needs that you can fill with new products and services.

Don't be afraid to experiment. Sam Walton continually tinkered with pricing, promotion and distribution strategies before hitting upon the combination that made Walmart the global success story it is today. Experimentation is key to finding the winning formula for success.

"THE SINGLE MOST IMPORTANT THING TO REMEMBER ABOUT ANY ENTERPRISE IS THAT THERE ARE NO RESULTS INSIDE ITS WALLS. THE RESULT OF A BUSINESS IS A SATISFIED CUSTOMER."

– Peter Drucker

8 Select the Right People for Your Team

As an entrepreneur with a Big Idea, you already have a number of skills that you need to succeed—innovation, commitment, and confidence. Another part of being successful is recognizing the skills that you lack and then hiring the right people to complement your team.

"I experienced this first hand when I started Successories. My former Creative Director, Mike McKee, brought not only his creative talents, but also his ideas and enthusiasm for my new venture. Together, we created an unstoppable team."

They say that the "whole is the sum of its parts." That's never been more true than in business, where someone else's passion may be just what's needed to do what you cannot do well.

Look for those who share your values and your vision. Working together, with a passion for the same cause, will prove to be an unbeatable combination.

"I HIRE PEOPLE BRIGHTER THAN ME AND THEN I GET OUT OF THEIR WAY."

– Lee Iacocca

9 Value Your Employees

Southwest Airlines' former CEO Herb Kelleher said it best, "*You have to treat your employees like customers,*" he told *Fortune* in 2001. "*When you treat them right, then they will treat your outside customers right.*"

While there's no arguing that equitable compensation and benefits are at the top of any employee's list, to keep your employees motivated, you need to make them feel valued and recognized for their contributions. As a small business owner, you're in a unique position to offer life/work balance perks, seek input on business tactics, provide opportunities for people to grow in their jobs, express appreciation for a job well done, and most of all to treat everyone with respect and dignity.

"EVERYONE WANTS TO FEEL THAT THE HOURS THAT THEY SPEND EVERY DAY AT WORK MATTER. SO LET YOUR TEAM MEMBERS KNOW THE VALUE OF THEIR CONTRIBUTIONS IN MAKING YOUR BUSINESS A SUCCESS."

– Peter Drucker

10 Persistence Wins the Race

Launching your Big Idea is just the beginning of your success as an entrepreneur. There will be many obstacles along the way, some of which you expect to encounter…and some which will blindside you. Each entrepreneur profiled in this book held the courage of his or her convictions and didn't give up when times got rough.

Fred Smith had to overcome a number of hurdles to get Federal Express off the ground, literally! Whether it was governmental regulations, rocky starts with investors or cash flow problems, Fred hung in there. Despite taking 26 months to break even, Fred knew his overnight package delivery business model was a winner. Each day, millions of individuals and businesses prove him right.

Perseverance is the real test of success for new business owners. You've already created your Big Idea, so plan your strategy, surround yourself with those who are as passionate as you are, and work through the challenges one by one. Success is there for the taking… if you persevere.

> "MOST PEOPLE GIVE UP JUST WHEN THEY'RE ABOUT TO ACHIEVE SUCCESS. THEY QUIT ON THE ONE YARD LINE. THEY GIVE UP AT THE LAST MINUTE OF THE GAME ONE FOOT FROM A WINNING TOUCH DOWN."
>
> *– H. Ross Perot*

ONE IDEA... JUST ONE, CAN CHANGE YOUR BUSINESS AND YOUR LIFE

It is my hope that this little book will "spark your imagination" into action. But, just a reminder... keep it close and read it often, because most of the time, Big Ideas don't come cascading like Niagara Falls. They usually are born one drop at a time.

Here's wishing you success on your quest for your Big Idea!

Mac Anderson
Founder, Simple Truths

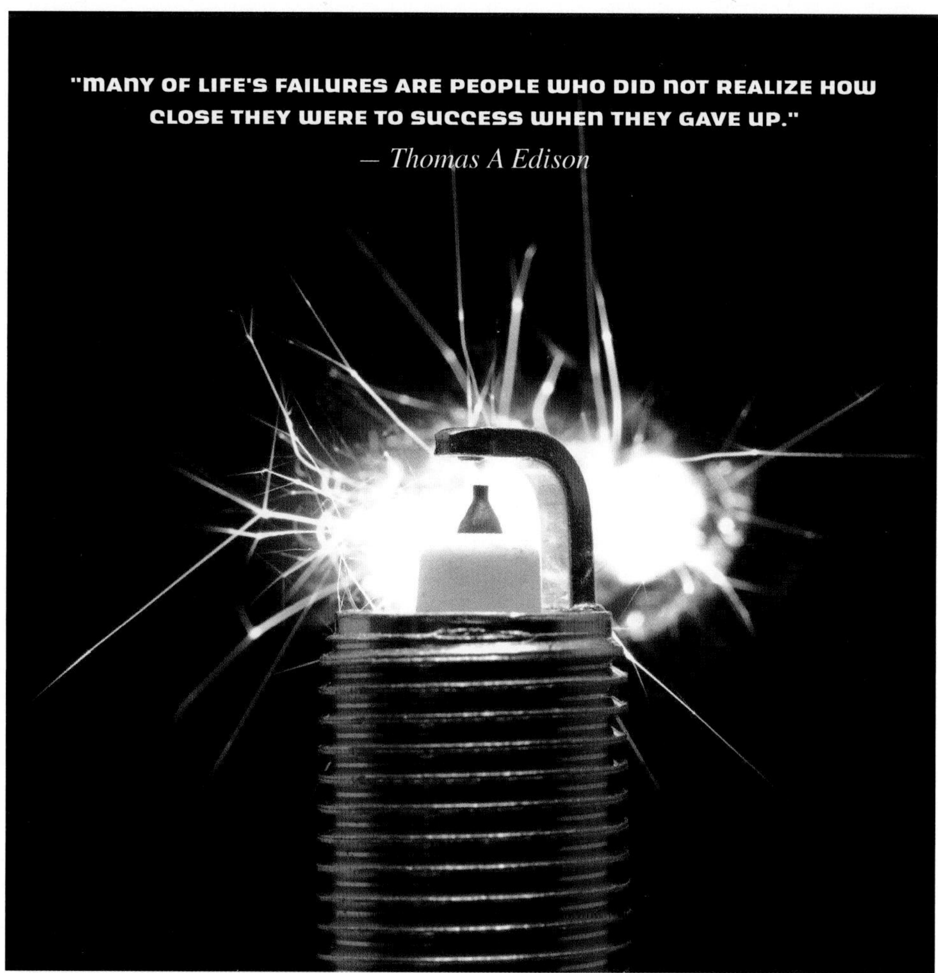
"MANY OF LIFE'S FAILURES ARE PEOPLE WHO DID NOT REALIZE HOW CLOSE THEY WERE TO SUCCESS WHEN THEY GAVE UP."
– Thomas A Edison

Mac Anderson

Mac Anderson is the founder of Simple Truths and Successories, Inc., the leader in designing and marketing products for motivation and recognition. These companies, however, are not the first success stories for Mac. He was also the founder and CEO of McCord Travel, the largest travel company in the Midwest, and part owner/VP of sales and marketing for Orval Kent Food Company, the country's largest manufacturer of prepared salads.

His accomplishments in these unrelated industries provide some insight into his passion and leadership skills. He also brings the same passion to his speaking where he speaks to many corporate audiences on a variety of topics, including leadership, motivation, and team building.

Mac has authored or co-authored fourteen books that have sold over three million copies. His titles include:

- Charging the Human Battery
- Customer Love
- Motivational Quotes
- Finding Joy
- You Can't Send a Duck to Eagle School
- 212°: The Extra Degree
- Learning to Dance in the Rain
- Change is Good ... You Go First
- The Nature of Success
- The Power of Attitude
- The Power of Kindness
- The Essence of Leadership
- To a Child, Love is Spelled T-I-M-E
- The Dash

For more information about Mac, visit www.simpletruths.com

If you have enjoyed this book we invite you to check out our entire collection of gift books, with free inspirational movies, at **www.simpletruths.com**

You'll discover it's a great way to inspire ***friends*** and ***family,*** or to thank your best ***customers*** and ***employees.***

We would love to hear how Simple Truths books enrich your life and others around you. Please send your comments to:

Simple Truths Feedback
1952 McDowell Road, Suite 300
Naperville, IL 60563
Or e-mails us at: comments@simpletruths.com

Or call us toll free...

800-900-3427

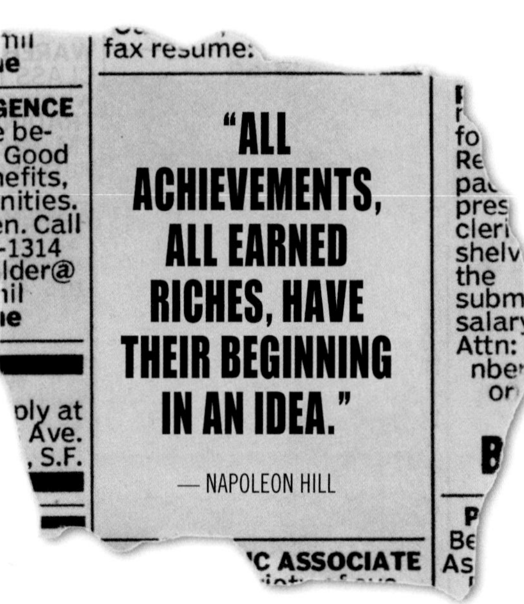

fax resume:
"ALL ACHIEVEMENTS, ALL EARNED RICHES, HAVE THEIR BEGINNING IN AN IDEA."
— NAPOLEON HILL
ASSOCIATE